AMERICAN
POPULAR ENTERTAINMENTS

THE AMERICAN DRAMA LIBRARY

The American Drama Library is an ongoing series of American plays in anthology format, in which we plan to emphasize nineteenth and early twentieth century plays. Each volume will be edited by a specialist in the field, with the purpose of revisioning a particular genre, historical perspective, or individual playwright. The greater portion of the plays will be those which are previously unpublished, out-of-print, or difficult to find.

Much of our dramatic past has been ignored, belittled, or misunderstood, with the result that dramatic literature as a genre has not taken its rightful place in American letters. A serious loss in the study of American drama is the unavailability of published plays, and the commentary on them by which an art form and its audience interrogates itself and its responses to social and artistic change, from an historical point of view. This is the all-important process by which a field of study matures in relationship to the new ideas of any age. It is also the basis from which a dramatic repertoire grows.

The American Drama Library will, we believe, bring many more plays, new interpretations of dramatic form and cultural history, and reconsideration of literary reputations to our readers. Perhaps in the reflection of American experience this new material gives back to us, we may see in greater detail how, as a society, we give form to our feelings in the art of drama.

The Publishers

AMERICAN POPULAR ENTERTAINMENTS

Jokes, Monologues, Bits, and Sketches

Edited, with an Introduction, by
Brooks McNamara

**PERFORMING ARTS JOURNAL PUBLICATIONS
NEW YORK CITY**

General Editors of The American Drama Library series:

Bonnie Marranca and Gautam Dasgupta

Library of Congress Cataloging in Publication Data
American Popular Entertainments
Library of Congress Catalog Card No.: 83-61192
ISBN: 0-933826-36-2 (cloth)
ISBN: 0-933826-37-0 (paper)

Graphic Design: Gautam Dasgupta

Printed in the United States of America

Publication of this book has been made possible in part by grants received from the National Endowment for the Arts, Washington, D.C., a federal agency, and the New York State Council on the Arts.

To Mae and Bob Noell
and
To The Memory of
"Greasy" Medlin
and
Lois Madden

Contents

THE DIALOGUE AND THE BIT

Acknowledgements

Material of the sort contained in this book is not always easy to locate, and I am most grateful to several friends who supplied me with sources, among them James Brown, Jerry Crawford, Paul Antonie Distler, William Elwood, Glenn Loney, and John Towsen. I owe a particular debt of gratitude to Louis Rachow, librarian of the Hampden-Booth Library and Theatre Collection at The Players, who made the Chuck Callahan Collection available to me. Performers who graciously allowed me to reprint their acts include Fred Bloodgood, Dale Madden and the late Lois Madden, Anna Blair Miller, and the late Julian "Greasy" Medlin. Barbara Kirshenblatt-Gimblett and Cynthia Jenner offered valuable ideas and suggestions. My assistant Sheyne Mueller cheerfully typed out what must have seemed to be an endless number of old acts, and also offered helpful suggestions along the way. I must also thank three friends who had nothing and everything to do with the creation of this book: Ralph Allen, Laurence Senelick and Don Wilmeth. Without the insights I have gained from them and from their pioneering work in the study of popular entertainment, this collection would never have come to be.

To The Reader

I have drawn on three kinds of sources for this collection: my own tapes of routines by old performers; manuscript material assembled by showmen for their own use; and printed texts, including the so-called "gagbooks" sold to professional performers (collections of jokes, monologues, bits, sketches, and the like), which were published during the last quarter of the nineteenth century and the first thirty years or so of the twentieth.

The organization of the anthology, in fact, is adapted from that of a typical gagbook. Most gagbooks arranged routines generically, in categories loosely based on the number of performers needed to present a particular kind of routine. For example, a gagbook in my own collection contains sections devoted to "monologues, acts for two males, acts for male and female, acts for four characters, sidewalk patter, parodies, poems, minstrelsy, farce, miscellaneous." Another features divisions into "monologues, sketches, acts, parodies, farces, minstrel first-parts, and afterpieces."

This organization based on the gagbooks reflects fairly accurately the major types of stock material which were associated with the popular stage. Others interested in the subject might prefer a somewhat different organization, but the one used here at least has the logic of tradition behind it—it probably reflects as clearly as any other organizational scheme the way in which the performers themselves conceived of the material.

I have not arranged material by entertainment form (vaudeville, burlesque, medicine show, and so on) since variations of the same routines invariably appeared in many different forms. I have, however, indicated in the Table of Contents the entertainment form with which the particular version published here was probably most closely connected. Where I am not certain about the source of a routine, I have followed my attribution with a question mark. I am almost *never* certain about dates. As is the case with much traditional literary material, the year in which a piece of work was first created is usually not known—even by those who performed it. In some cases we do know the year in which an item was collected or published, but such a date tells us little about the actual age of a piece. Generally speaking, I believe that most of the material included here was in use between about 1850 and 1930, but some of it is clearly much older.

By the same token, I do not generally know who originated these routines. A burlesque comic named Chuck Callahan, for example, set down on paper several hundred acts of all kinds. Callahan probably did not think of himself as the originator of the material, however, but simply as a kind of scribe who recorded traditional routines for possible later use. In fact, many of those who claimed to have written a particular piece of material were also merely scribes who felt that there was some economic advantage in establishing authorship. The proprietors of gagbooks and minstrel guides often fell into this category.

The words and phrases which show people used when referring to their acts present some problems for the reader—especially those terms connected with comedy routines involving two or more performers. There is no consistency about the way that these routines were labeled by entertainers. Most medicine show people, for example, referred to a short, simple comedy routine as a "bit," and a longer, more elaborate one as an "act" or "nigger act" (even when the routine was not done in blackface), or an "afterpiece" (even when the act did not appear last on the evening's bill). Burlesque performers, on the other hand, tended to call every comedy scene a "bit." But, as theatre historian Ralph Allen suggests, burlesquers subdivided it into "the 'flirtation scene,' a short, single-joke situation which can be played in front of a downstage drop by no more than two or three men and two women; and the 'body scene'—a more extended bit with a complicated premise, designed for performance in a full-stage set by a cast of seven or eight."

Other entertainers used quite different words to describe these same types of routines: "sketch," "skit," "scene," "blackout," and "playlet," were also in common usage. The performers of the day seemed to have no particular difficulty understanding what was meant, but the modern reader is likely to be baffled by such casual use of terms. For this reason, I have tried to standardize terms in my Introduction and Notes, knowing full well that my choices represent misuse from the point of view of some old performers. Thus, I use "bit" to refer to a short, one-joke routine, and "sketch" to describe a somewhat more elaborate and developed one. I have also reserved the words "routine" and "act" for general use, to describe any piece of material of any sort presented by an entertainer on stage, whether language was involved or not. Here again, I am well aware that there are those who would use these words in a different way.

A note on the editing may be useful to the reader. With the exception of items which I have transcribed from tapes, the material in this anthology appears essentially as it was originally written down. I have standardized the form in which dialogue is presented, but I have not changed the majority of grammatical errors. Punctuation has been regularized where it affects the sense of a line, and obvious errors have been corrected, but the texts are presented here basically as I found them. My transcriptions have been checked for accuracy with the entertainers whose material I recorded in performance.

One other point is probably worth making. Much of the material here is offensive to late-twentieth-century sensibilities—it is often frankly racist and denigrates women. But to leave out or even to minimize such material would be to misrepresent the course of American theatrical history. For that reason it is offered here "warts and all," in the hope that it will add to the understanding of traditional American humor and of the stock material so basic to our traditional popular theatre.

B. McN.

Introduction

No account of the Olympia [Music Hall] of that time (1898-1899) is complete without mentioning the lost art of the "afterpiece." At a rehearsal, the company decided on the skit that would conclude the performance. Would it be the "Irish Justice" or "The Ghost Walks," for example. Everyone knew the fundamental plots of these skits. It was their stock in trade. Some even had manuscripts of their own. . . . Though crude and ad-libbed the afterpiece was, nevertheless, an art form that grew among the performers and so had a very meaningful place in the theatre history of the time.

Rose Miller, *My First Love Wears Two Masks*

American entertainment of the late nineteenth and early twentieth centuries depended not only on the play, but on stock materials: the joke in all of its forms; the monologue; the pitch; the lecture; the dialogue; the bit, a short one-joke scene; and the sketch, a longer, more elaborate scene or playlet. These were the building blocks from which many of our traditional entertainments were constructed, and it is on variations of this stock material that I have focused this anthology. Among the variations are classics such as "Three O'Clock Train" and "A Deck of Cards," which were used over and over again in different types of entertainment. A few such routines are occasionally still performed today by old entertainers. Others may be seen in early films or heard on recordings of radio programs. But most of the items included here are virtually unknown to students and scholars of American theatre. They deserve to be studied and understood, however, because they represent an important lost segment of our theatrical past.

Showmen, like the poor, are always with us. From the seventeenth century onward, colonial taverns and market squares were the gathering places of itinerant conjurers, performing mountebanks, freaks, and animal trainers. In court houses, converted store buildings and jury-rigged theatres, colonists were treated to the wonders of the "Philosophical Optical Machine," the

"Celebrated Lecture on Heads," and a boy of seven who "dances and capers upon the strait roap and a woman who dances a corant and a jigg with baskets on her feet and iron fetters on her legs." It was only later, however, that popular entertainment became both a big business and a central institution in American life. During the first half of the nineteenth century, the American worker gained more leisure and greater affluence, at the same time that traditional religious biases against performance were breaking down. Improved transportation allowed showmen to move into previously inaccessible rural areas, and the growth of sizeable towns meant that adequate theatre buildings were more often available. Thus, by 1850, there was a considerable potential audience for live performance and an increasing body of showmen and performers who were eager to respond to the developing need for popular entertainment.

The line between these popular forms and what later came to be called "legitimate" theatre was not always very clear in the nineteenth century. Knockabout farces shared the stage with the works of classic authors, and performers like Edwin Booth, whose career was built around Shakespeare, also acted as a matter of course in popular comedies and melodramas. There was, however, a more-or-less definable group of truly popular entertainments, aimed at a broad, relatively unsophisticated audience, which had little interest in art but a great hunger for entertainment. It was in many ways a precursor to the mass audience that began to develop at the turn of the century with the growth of the American film.

From 1840 onward through about 1940 several related forms of live entertainment emerged which were aimed directly at the tastes and the pocketbooks of the ordinary American. Among them was the circus, perhaps the best known popular form today. European-style single-ring circuses were seen in large American cities as early as the eighteenth century. The touring tent circus, however, was a nineteenth-century innovation, and its distinctive three-ring form was a post-Civil War development. In the period from about 1870 to 1920 the circus developed as perhaps the premiere American entertainment institution, its fortunes bound up with the burgeoning American advertising industry and the growth of the nation's great railroad network, which it came to employ as a method of transport.

By the twenties, however, the famous circus street parade had largely disappeared, and motion pictures, radio and the generally increased mobility of the average American had begun to spell the form's decline. Its close cousin, the Wild West show, a circus-like celebration of Western life and adventure, first developed by Buffalo Bill Cody in 1883, had virtually vanished by 1930, a victim of the Western movie and the Depression.

That peculiarly American entertainment form, the minstrel show, arose in the 1840s and, for a quarter of a century, was both popular with audiences and an important influence on the work of performers in other branches of show business. In its early years, it was essentially a simple variety show built around white performers in blackface who presented comedy and songs in Negro dialect. After the Civil War, minstrel companies featuring black performers began to be seen in many areas. These companies were to provide an entree into show business for many blacks and to become an important influence on the form and content of more recent black show business.

In later years, as the novelty wore off and competition from other types of entertainment increased, blackface minstrelsy became more elaborate and more expensive to mount and transport. In a desperate bid for audiences, managers created "Hibernian" minstrels, all-girl companies, and a number of other eccentric variations that bore little resemblance to the traditional shows. But nobody seemed particularly interested, and by 1900 there were only a handful of white minstrel companies left on the road. Much of their traditional material, however, had been absorbed into other kinds of popular entertainment such as vaudeville, burlesque and the medicine show. In later years, minstrel characters, music and comedy routines were also to influence the Broadway revue (most spectacularly with Al Jolson and Eddie Cantor), as well as film, radio, and even television, where "Amos and Andy" was still to be seen as late as the fifties.

The traveling medicine show developed in the years after the Civil War and continued in some rural areas as late as World War II. A typical show was nothing more than an evening of miscellaneous entertainment, often presented in the open air, which borrowed from the circus, the Wild West show, minstrelsy, and in later years from vaudeville. It was unique among forms of popular entertainment because the profits did not come from box office receipts—most medicine shows, in fact, had no admission charge—but from the sale of patent medicine. The medicine sales, conducted by a staff "pitchman" who sometimes claimed to be a physician, were inserted at various points in the show much like the commercials in later radio and television.

Another rural entertainment was the so-called repertoire company, which performed under canvas like a circus, as well as in the many small town "opera houses" built in the nineteenth century. Among the shows presented by rep companies were popular comedies and classic melodramas such as *The Two Orphans*, *The Octoroon*, and *East Lynne*, usually with vaudeville specialties nestled between the acts. Some companies featured a stock "rube" character called Toby, who was inserted in the plays; others performed only *Uncle Tom's Cabin* for years at a time. As late as the 1950s a few companies continued to tour out-of-the-way parts of the Middle West. But the great age of the touring rep show, like that of the medicine show, had ended with World War II, when rationing of gasoline and tires, together with staff shortages and increasing competition from radio and the movies, had sounded the death knell of the form.

The commercial viability of spotless family entertainment with educational overtones was first demonstrated by P. T. Barnum in the 1840s at his famous

American Museum in New York. The "moral and educational" premise which he pioneered later became a much touted feature of circus and traveling carnival advertising. The quintessence of such an approach, however, lay not with the circus but with tent chautauqua, a small-town institution that developed toward the end of the century and had largely disappeared by 1930. Stemming originally from the educational and religious summer programs given at Lake Chautauqua, New York, and from the tradition of the lyceum, a kind of nineteenth-century speakers' bureau, touring chautauqua under canvas ultimately became a sort of high-minded vaudeville, treating small-town audiences to the triumvirate of "entertainment, education and inspiration."

In the cities, during the same period, vaudeville had also won for itself a family audience. During the eighties and nineties showmen were enthusiastically transforming the rough and tumble shows found in male-oriented "concert saloons" and "variety halls" into more respectable—and often more profitable—vaudeville entertainments. By the nineties, a broadly based "clean vaudeville," with appeal to all classes, had become a major form of urban entertainment. Theatres for the new family medium sprang up across the country and performers from such forms as minstrelsy, the circus and the medicine show found an appealing new market for their traditional acts. Huge circuits of vaudeville theatres were established, and the amount of material needed for the circuits continued to increase as the years wore on. One early solution was to include motion pictures on vaudeville bills. By the teens, of course, the motion picture theatre—with or without vaudeville between the films—had become common, and the thirties saw the movie industry come into its own with the talking film. These developments, together with the growth of radio and the tight-money period of the Depression, eventually spelled the end of one of America's most widespread live entertainment forms.

Vaudeville's cousin, burlesque, was also involved with the concert saloons and variety halls. By the 1870s, showmen had begun to combine material from English burlesque with these "honky-tonk" entertainments and with the structure of the minstrel shows to create a distinctive kind of theatrical performance in which racy jokes and comedy routines were alternated with song and dance numbers featuring scantily clad women. In the first years of the twentieth century, burlesque circuits or "wheels" sprang up around the country and the form became big business. The early twentieth-century shows were, for the most part, bawdy but by no means obscene. By the 1930s, however, burlesque comedy had become increasingly scatalogical and the "striptease" aspect of the shows increasingly prominent. By 1942 burlesque had been outlawed in New York City, and the form declined badly from that point on. But a few small independent burlesque houses were still to be found in American cities as late as the 1970s.

Until recently historians have paid little attention to these popular entertainments. Within the last decade or so, however, scholars have begun to interest themselves in the complex relationships among traditional performance modes. In 1973, for example, theatre historian Garff Wilson briefly charted some of the main connections among major types of American entertainment. "The circus," Wilson wrote, "borrowed blackface entertainment from minstrelsy, horseback performances from the equestrian drama, and variety acts from vaudeville. Vaudeville adopted blackface numbers from minstrelsy, leg shows from burlesque, and acrobatics and animal acts from the circus. In fact, all the types of popular theatre are basically a series of specialties strung together in a characteristic way. Each emphasizes a slightly different specialty, but each aims to satisfy the tastes of a polyglot audience by providing novel and varied entertainment which is easily understood."

But Wilson's shrewd analysis may be taken one step farther. Underlying all of these complicated trade-offs and transformations lay a shared body of traditional stock material which has scarcely been explored—and which, by and large, is scarcely even known to exist. As more information emerges about American popular performance, however, it becomes possible to lay out something about the evolution and the function of this tradition.

All of the traditional entertainments mentioned by Wilson depended on stock material, and all were organized according to a "variety structure." That is, they were made up of a number of independent acts which were assembled into a show. Unlike the acts in a conventional play, the acts that made up these entertainments generally had little or no thematic or plot relationship to one another. Although they might be bound together by some simple bracketing device such as the blackface convention of minstrelsy, the organization of acts on a bill was governed by practical considerations about balancing the elements of a show, by traditions about the location of certain kinds of material within the show's framework, and by the attempt to create a "rising action" as the evening progressed, building toward a climactic act at or near the end of the show.

Consider, for example, the organization of the mid-nineteenth century minstrel show. Usually there were three distinct sections. The first of these involved a line-up of the company, with the Middleman or Interlocutor at the center of the stage, flanked on either side by the singer-musicians and Tambo and Bones, the Endmen. This so-called First Part featured songs by the company and a barrage of jokes (sometimes called a "crossfire") among Interlocutor, Tambo and Bones. It finished with a "cakewalk" finale, during which each member of the company presented a brief musical or dance specialty. The Second Part or "olio" offered longer specialty numbers, and the Third Part was generally an afterpiece, a sketch or short play involving some or all of the company—perhaps a burlesque of Shakespeare or some other serious author, or a brief musical comedy about life in the Old South called a "plantation scene."

Of course, there were countless variations on this format. But the basic structural device of a section devoted to a melange of jokes, songs, and dances, followed by lengthier specialties and an afterpiece designed to show off the whole company, offered performers a familiar and convenient framework on which to hang both old and new material. Within this framework the performers and the organizer of the show were free to create the individual parts—and the entire bill—through their choice of jokes, songs, dances, comedy routines and afterpiece material.

This minstrel approach was a traditional one, basically not very different from that employed in Renaissance Italy by the actors of the *commedia dell'arte.* "As in the *commedia,*" theatre historian Richard Moody suggests, "the special talents of the acting company determined the specific nature of the performance. Any limitations suggested by the script were observed only, if compatible with the creative desires of the particular players. . . . The specialty numbers of the Negro-minstrel routine were in a way comparable to the interpolated comic routines, the *lazzi,* of the *commedia.* And, like the *commedia,* the minstrel show depended for its success on the talents of the performers and not on a prepared script."

A similarly stable yet flexible format also served as the organizing principle behind several other types of American popular entertainment. Some borrowed their structure directly from the circus or the minstrel show, adapting these forms as necessary to their own requirements. Others employed similar structures to encompass a number of essentially unrelated or only casually related acts.

An 1884 program from Tony Pastor's New Fourteenth Street Theatre offers a useful example of how such a structure actually operated in early vaudeville. The program indicates that an overture was followed by a bit or sketch of some sort, probably a brief burlesque melodrama, called "Ye Murder at ye Old Toll House; or, Ye Dog of Weehawken," with a cast of half a dozen. Next came a female singer and a marionette company, presenting a "Fairy Pantomime, BEAUTY AND THE BEAST and HUMPTY DUMPTY, introducing the Animated Skeleton and Magic Turk, making a complete entertainment in miniature." The marionettes were followed by the De Bar Brothers in "their Elastic, Agile, India Rubber Serpentine Manipulations of Contortionism," and what was probably the closing number of the first half, a comic song routine by Pastor himself.

The second half opened with a classic bit or sketch called "A Subject for Dissection." Next came a pair of female singers in "Musical Sketches" of some kind, followed by the legendary McIntyre and Heath in a blackface act complete with "PLANTATION DANCING." They were followed by a "Skipping Rope Song and Dance and Bell Hoop Exercises," and a musical bit or sketch known as "The Widow De Witt." The show's climax was evidently a short play, a five-scene afterpiece with a rural setting, called "Mrs. Partington," which included live animals and an "old fashioned dance." The finale was billed as "the last GRAND CLIMAX OF FUN, 'THOSE

STAIRS.' "

The variety structure found in Pastor's show was replicated countless times in other types of popular entertainment. Its absolute simplicity made the structure especially appealing to managers. In essence, the format of the show generally amounted to the presentation of one or more specialty acts by each entertainer on the bill, plus several bits and sketches in which a number of entertainers—or perhaps the whole company—performed. The resulting show was relatively cheap and efficient to run in comparison to legitimate theatre, in no small part because it could be varied considerably according to the available performers and their particular talents. Unlike legitimate companies, which depended for their existence on the ability to cast and mount particular plays, the producers of variety entertainments had the freedom to restructure a show completely as circumstances dictated.

Given a group of seasoned performers, the possibilities were almost limitless. The amount of material which some performers accumulated was little short of staggering. An old burlesque comic claimed to be able to perform 300 scenes on the spot and twice that number with a single day's notice. His claims may have been a bit fanciful, but it is true that most performers were required by the very nature of their work to offer managers a substantial repertoire. A tent show specialty performer, for example, needed at least eight different routines in order to present a new act for each matinee and evening performance, and many medicine show entertainers were required to "change for a week" or "change strong for ten nights." But finding material was relatively easy since performers often worked in a number of different kinds of entertainment during their careers, picking up useful jokes, songs, monologues, bits and sketches wherever they were to be found.

A performer named Anna Mae Noell once wrote to me about her family's involvement in various kinds of entertainment. Her story is by no means an unusual one. "I lay awake part of the night," she wrote, "thinking of the old days, and was surprised at the many areas of show business that my parents had been connected with: 1. Medicine shows (barnstorming and outdoor shows). 2. Tent dramatics (*Girl of the Golden West, Ten Nights in a Barroom, Way Down East*, etc.). 3. Carnival under canvas (stage acts). 4. Outdoor carnival (stage acts). 5. Circus side show (stage acts). 6. Indoor side show (stage acts). 7. Hubert's dime museum in New York (stage acts). 8. Vaudeville revues . . . Oh! Almost forgot—Dad had an animal show after he married my stepmother." Families like Mae's came to know all of the classic stock material associated with each kind of popular entertainment. Some performers created homemade gagbooks filled with clippings and notes about potentially useful routines. Others assembled whole libraries of professional gagbooks, minstrel guides, manuscripts, and published acts of all sorts. Out of necessity, performers became skilled at adapting this storehouse of material to each new type of show in which they played.

The origins of much of this traditional popular material are misty and uncertain. One suspects that a good many acts—like the structure that encompassed them—had their source in the circus or minstrel show, both of which clearly provided considerable material for other forms of entertainment. But there is often no obvious connection to the circus or minstrelsy, and even when there is, it is not certain that material actually originated in one or the other of these forms. It is likely that many pieces may be traced to English circus, fairground or music hall routines—and perhaps much farther back in time and to other nations as well. An ultimate connection with, say, the *commedia* is unproved and probably unprovable, but it is easy to see important similarities in both form and content that span the centuries.

It is sometimes possible to locate an author for what may be the earliest version of some classic act. But in the normal course of things, authorship, like strict adherence to a particular text, was of no real concern to traditional entertainers. Theirs was a theatre of oral tradition, and fanciful stories abounded among old performers about how this act or that one originated. The son of an old medicine show entertainer, for example, recalled "The Three O'Clock Train" as "an act of such hoary origin that it was originally titled 'The Three O'Clock Coach,' and a version of it is known to have been played by a medicine show traveling through Michigan and Ontario way back in 1827." He may well have been right, but nobody really cared very much. The material was there to be used, and used it was in whatever happened to be the most immediate and effective form.

This is not to suggest that out-and-out piracy of another entertainer's act was viewed favorably by most show people. Quite the contrary; some vaudeville performers, for example, might use precisely the same act for years at a time, and violently resented the theft of their carefully worked-out routines. But much material was conceived to be in a kind of show business public domain and was free for the taking by any performer who fancied it.

Such stock material, of course, was constantly being reshaped. For example, a minstrel monologue, performed in blackface with a heavy Negro accent, might appear elsewhere as, say, an Irish monologue, done in a totally different makeup and accent and with some of the references altered to make an Irish context more or less credible. As the monologue came to be known by other performers, new elements might be added to bring it up to date or to focus it in some way for a special audience. Thus, a burlesque version might retain some of the elements of the original minstrel piece while adding sexual gags and by-play. A chautauqua version of the same monologue, however, would be spotlessly laundered for conservative family audiences. Local jokes might also be added, or the expressions and rhythms of language altered to tailor material for a regional audience.

Under time pressure some expendable segments of the monologue might be dropped—or, conversely, random jokes or pieces of other acts could be added to stretch it. The old monologue might even be broken up among several speakers and elaborated into a bit or sketch or even a fully developed play. Or it might be reduced to a single joke, or perhaps set to music and used as a song in some other routine.

Like Richard Moody, historian Ralph Allen draws on the image of the *commedia dell'arte* in explaining the loose structure of the comedy routines which were a staple of American burlesque. The burlesque routine, Allen says, "bears a striking resemblance to the *sogetto* of the *commedia dell'arte*. It is an outline of the action, a frame into which the comedian inserts his own eccentric character, his own pieces of business (his *lazzi*, if you will) and some of his own stock speeches (his *concetti*)."

Much the same principle may be seen with medicine show bits and sketches. Some years ago, when I wrote a book on the medicine show, I decided that I wanted to include several of these stock acts as appendices. The old medicine show performer, Anna Mae Noell, kindly agreed to write out some samples from memory. I found the scripts which Mae sent to me disappointing at first since they were fragmentary and often apparently incoherent.

I later came to realize how wrong my first impression had been. Over the next several years I was able to see a number of the bits and sketches performed by Mae herself and other old entertainers. Onstage, it quickly became clear that her texts were not half-remembered fragments, as I had imagined, but scenarios. Mae had set down on paper little more than the traditional outlines for action familiar to all medicine show performers of the day. These outlines were complete only when fleshed out and reshaped by the performers, who inserted a store of familiar jokes, poems, dances and songs. It was only onstage that the real shape and texture of the acts eventually became clear.

Thus I came to see that the references in Mae's texts to "Business," "Lots of funny business here," "the Straight fusses," and so on, were not products of a faulty memory or merely bad writing, but were conventional instructions to the actors to improvise, using some traditional speech or business, in order to create a bridge to the next set piece of dialogue. Even the "set" dialogue, I discovered, was by no means inviolable in performance; the actors worked with the logic or sense of many lines rather than with an exact reading of them. It became clear that only certain comedy punch lines were delivered in almost exactly the same way at each performance—and then only because a particular reading of these lines had been found by a performer to be more or less surefire. As Mae and others told me, this fluid approach to the text meant that even someone who did not know a particular act could learn it rapidly, often without a script, memorizing the main lines of the plot and enough of the dialogue to get by, while at the same time locating places where prized pieces of business might be inserted.

Traditional acts of all sorts were kept deliberately flexible—not only so that they could be custom tailored to fit any time limitations or to accommodate new material, but also so that they could incorporate the stock characters so much a part of the American popular entertainment of the day. Most medicine show bits and sketches, for example, centered on a figure known as

Jake or Sambo, a close relative of the minstrel comics. Although this figure was central, he was never very clearly drawn; it was assumed by all concerned that any performer doing the role would present his own particular Jake, complete with his own personal material.

Much the same situation obtained with most other entertainers of the day; they played their specialties—a "Dutch" character, a comic Irishman, a blackface comic, a rube, a tramp, or a comic Jew, for example—and reorganized lines and situations as necessary to fit their own stock characters and their own personalities. "In popular entertainment," suggest historians Clifford Ashby and Suzanne May, "transmutability of character is more of a handicap than a virtue; audiences want an always-recognizable commodity, want to know what they're going to see before they purchase a ticket."

Even the playscript was viewed in a very different way by these entertainers. Although "legitimate" drama and the popular play employed the same basic conventions of playwriting and staging, a huge gulf separated the works of Bronson Howard, James A. Herne and Clyde Fitch from the farces of Harrigan and Hart, the ubiquitous touring productions of *Uncle Tom's Cabin*, and such standard melodramatic favorites as *Rescued from Highbinders*, *Queen of the White Slaves*, and *Midnight in Chinatown*. It was the difference between selfconscious art on the one hand and pure craft on the other; between the playwright as theatre artist and the playwright as showman; between the play as artistic creation and the play as a vehicle for traditional comic, melodramatic and spectacular devices. To the showman the playscript was a less-than-sacred document.

I own, for example, a crudely typed script of *Uncle Tom's Cabin*, probably from an early twentieth-century Tom show or tent rep company, which bears some revealing notes on its title page. Typed there are explanations of how to perform the play in different ways, using seven adults and one child, six adults and one child, and so on. There is a note about cutting the entire first scene of the show for casting reasons, as well as other notes throughout about cuts, additions, and other changes in the text to suit the company which was presenting the show. The script appears to be an arrangement of the famous George Aiken dramatization of Mrs. Stowe's novel, but clearly the Aiken version was only a jumping-off place. Such was the case with many standard plays when they came into the hands of touring rep companies. Alterations were made as required; vaudeville was usually inserted between the acts and even sometimes within the show itself; and plays were often revised to include one of several bucolic stock characters, the most famous of which was the red-headed yokel named Toby who, for many years, delighted audiences in the Middle West with his improvised antics. In fact, as Ashby and May suggest, there was very good reason for such an approach. On the tent shows, they write, "actors were woefully underrehearsed and far from perfect in their lines, a condition which led to a casual regard for the words of the playwright. Typically the show rehearsed for a total of one week before opening a bill of six plays—plus vaudeville. As diligently as actors worked on their parts, there was simply no time to learn them exactly. This led to a semi-commedia style of playing in which the cast followed the general direction of the plot without knowing the exact lines.''

All of this suggests once again the remarkable adaptability of traditional live popular entertainments—and yet virtually none of these forms have survived down to our own time. One wonders how such a flexible and tenacious branch of the amusement business came to die. In no small part the answer seems to lie with the growth of the movies in the early years of the twentieth century. The motion picture had a great deal to offer the popular entertainment entrepreneur, both in terms of novelty and—perhaps even more important—in terms of economy and efficiency. The material seen live in comparatively few theatres could now be brought to audiences in many different locations, with relatively little trouble and at small cost to the showman, greatly increasing that mass audience which had been developing for half a century or more.

At the end of the nineteenth century, motion pictures were seen in vaudeville houses, in the theatres attached to dime museums, and in a host of small town "opera houses." They appeared out-of-doors and in the tents used by medicine showmen, concert companies and touring tent repertoire companies. A medicine show that played the town hall in Colebrook, New Hampshire, added E. S. Porter's famous film *Dream of a Rarebit Fiend* to their usual fare of singing, dancing, acrobatics and fire eating; and an itinerant showman named Augustus Rapp increasingly used films to fill up his bills when talent was in short supply. "I would add a two reel comedy to each of the programs," he said, "or some one night I might have an all picture show like *Uncle Tom's Cabin* or *Life of Christ*." Gradually the "all picture show" became more and more common in rural areas and traveling companies switched from live performance to motion picture presentations. There was every reason to do so. As an old medicine showman suggested: "What chance has a med-man with big expenses, tons of equipment and seven to nine performers against a fellow who comes along with practically no output and carries his entire show, actors, wardrobe and scenery, in a tin can?''

Of course, the medicine man was right. The movies were a more efficient medium than live popular entertainment, and they were already well on their way to destroying the older forms. The new nickelodeons springing up in the cities were gradually switching the emphasis from live entertainment with additional films to the reverse of that formula—or to movies with no live entertainment at all, standing alone on their own merits.

Although the old forms of live popular entertainment began to fade away in the early twentieth century, much traditional material continued to live in the motion picture. Many film actors came out of the popular entertainment tradition and they simply transferred their stock acts from stage to screen. "I discovered," wrote drama critic Alan Dale in 1916, "that the screens were the veritable scavengers of the amusement world, that they could be relied upon to remove from the theatre all that the theatre couldn't possibly want—things that it had ignobly fattened upon in less felicitous days—and that the 'legitimate' had never been able to rid itself of.''

Dale's rather arch message was clear: the movies had developed less as a radical new entertainment medium than as a continuation of the tradition of nineteenth-century popular entertainment which he, as a high-minded theatre critic, professed to scorn. Indeed, it is quite true that the motion pictures drew heavily in their first years on material from the already well established live amusement industry. Filmed vaudeville acts and material from popular melodramas and farces loomed large in the early days. Later the flow would slow considerably, but such stock material was still an influence on the movies as late as the sound era, and one encounters almost unalloyed stock bits and sketches in the films of such show business veterans as Abbott and Costello.

At the same time, other media had begun to provide additional possibilities for old showmen. The Broadway revue, which had been developing since the early years of the twentieth century, served as a new home for much traditional material. Al Jolson, for example, stepped directly from the minstrel stage to the stages of Broadway, and carried with him much of the traditional flavor of the older medium. But perhaps it was radio that became the real museum of American popular entertainment. Even more than the films, radio demanded a constant supply of fresh material, and much stock comedy was recycled by old showmen. In the radio—and later television—work of such favorites as Bob Hope, Jack Benny, Burns and Allen, Phil Silvers, and Gosden and Correll (''Amos and Andy'') may be seen a huge and virtually unexplored repository of traditional stock comedy. In more recent years, film, radio and television—like the demonic plant in the current hit show, *The Little Shop of Horrors*—have constantly cried out, ''Feed me!'' Material can no longer be used for decades at a time, and many of the classic routines have sunk with scarcely a trace in a new kind of amusement business with a ravenous appetite and no time to spare. On reflection, it seems that this new amusement business has almost certainly created its own stock classics. But that is another story.

Brooks McNamara

JOKES AND OTHER COMIC MATERIAL

The most basic sort of stock material consisted of jokes, quips, parodies of songs, facetious song introductions, and the like. These comic snippits, many of which had their origins outside the theatre, were often used as increments in all sorts of acts. Thus, a musical act might begin with a joke or two, employ comedy material as a kind of bridge between songs, or introduce the songs themselves with anachronistic titles: "I'd like to sing you a little song called 'She Used to be a Soldier's Sweetheart, But Now She's an Officer's Mess.' " Certain jokes and song parodies became standard fixtures of many acts, but of course the point is that fresh material could be inserted in an act at the pleasure of the performers and removed again or shifted about if the effect was not right.

Alternatively, an act might actually be built out of a selection of jokes and related comic material. In its simplest form such an act could be nothing more than a string of miscellaneous gags told by a single performer or perhaps split up between two. In a somewhat more structured approach the performers might develop a single theme, as was often the case with the "crossfire" between the Interlocutor and the minstrel endmen, Tambo and Bones. Termagant wives, mothers-in-law, and the idiosyncrasies of various ethnic groups were all classics. In many instances this approach moved in the direction of a fully developed monologue or bit.

Some jokes and related items began their lives as children's rhymes or riddles, or as other types of oral tradition literature which are still familiar to us today. Much was also borrowed from the acts of other entertainers, although a number of show people took part of their material from published joke books or subscribed to the many gagbooks and newsletters put out especially for showmen. The most famous of these was "Madison's Budget," a paperbound annual, first published in 1870, containing a wide range of jokes, monologues, dialogues, and sketch material, and selling for a dollar. But dozens, perhaps hundreds of other gagbooks were issued over the years, most of them providing the same basic sort of material.

Often they were humble ventures, no more than crudely dittoed typescripts with only cursory attention given to the niceties of punctuation and spelling.

But they served a vital function. The proprietor of "Uncle Cal's Manuscript No. 7" advised show people that "The compiler of this collection does not claim to be the originator of the material herein contained. It is taken from his private library, and he has used all this material, on the stage and in radio. You are receiving the fruits of a life-time in the theatrical business. Some of these gags and situation comedy, you may think, are old-fashioned or stale; but listen to any of our popular comedians and you will hear the same jokes but with a different twist. It's a wise joke that knows its own father."

The majority of the material in this section is taken from an early twentieth-century gagbook in my collection, although two items come from routines presented by old showmen, which I recorded at the 1981 Folklife Festival at the Smithsonian Institution. In selecting items I have tried to provide an example or two from each major category of stock gag material used by American entertainers. The song parodies are, perhaps, of special interest since they are part of a central tradition in popular entertainment. Parodies or burlesques of plays, novels, songs (and later motion picture and radio shows) were a regular feature of popular performance, and examples of other kinds of parody material appear throughout this anthology.

The "drift" of gag material from one medium to another is suggested by the joke beginning, "My girl is so fat . . . ," which is perhaps most familiar today as a popular song of the forties called "A-Huggin' and A-Chalkin'." The item which ends this section is not a single joke, but, in fact, a string of brief gags, casually organized around two classic subjects of popular stage comedy, mothers-in-law and fat ladies. With such an organization the entertainer was moving in the direction of the full-scale monologue, examples of which are found in the next section.

The shades of night were falling fast,
When for a kiss he asked her;
She must have answered "Yes" because
The shades came down much faster.

Well, yesterday I took Mother and Lizzie, she's my best girl, downtown. While we were down there, Lizzie kept saying that she wanted to eat. After a while Mother said, "Well, Henry, it looks like you will have to feed us." I says, "All right," and went into one of those new fangled restaurants. Boy, do they have some new ideas. When you give your order for food, you don't order in the regular way; if you want steak, when the waiter comes, you just look at him and say, "Steak me." If you want a bowl of soup, why you just say, "Soup me." Boy, was that Lizzie starved—that is, from the way she talked. Well, finally the waiter come round and I decided that I wanted a steak, so I looked up at the waiter and said, "Steak me." Mother, she wanted fish, so she looked up at the waiter and said, "Fish me." The waiter looked over at Lizzie, and I nearly fell out of my seat—she said she was not hungry, did not want a thing. We insisted, but she would not eat a bite. After we finished, we got out on the street and I said to Lizzie, "Honey, why didn't you order something to eat? She just looked at me and said, "Not on your life, boy, I just wanted a glass of milk." Take your time, folks. I'll wait; let it sink in.

Snow is white and coal is black.
If your pants are loose, pull in the slack.

A skunk sat on a stump. The skunk thunk the stump stunk and
the stump thunk the skunk stunk.

I hate skunks, they put on such awful airs.

It's sweet to love, but oh how bitter,
To love a girl and then not git her.
I lay my head on a railroad track;
A train come along so I pulled it back.

To the tune of "My Bonnie Lies Over the Ocean"
  Last night as I lay on my pillow,
  Last night as I lay on my bed.
  I stuck both my feet out the window,
  (Pause) Next morning the neighbors were dead.

A baby is an alimentary canal with a loud voice at one end
and no responsibility at the other.

My sweetheart calls me "Nero" cause I fiddle around so much.

Did you ever hear about the butcher who backed into the meat grinder and got a little behind in his orders?

My girl is so fat, that when I go to see her, I take a piece of chalk along with me. I hug her by reaching as far as I can, and then I make a mark. Then I start at the mark and go another arm's length. (*Laugh.*) It takes just nine marks to get around her. (*Pause.*) Last night when I hugged her I met [local name] coming around the other side.

I wish I were a little bird.
Up in the sky so blue.
I'd fly up o'er my teacher's head
(*Pause*) You know what birdies do.

Hokum Song: Any Four Bar Vamp for Melody

1 — I've got a gal, her name is Liz,
   Not good looking, an awful fizz
   Arm like a blacksmith, foot like a ham,
   Dumb as a mule from Alabam'.
2 — Warts on her neck, big as an egg,
   Hump on her back, has one cork leg.
   One eye is green, the other blue.
   Her hair is false, her teeth are too.
3 — Underslung jaw, her mouth is mum.
   All out of whack from chewing gum.
   Turned up nose, and Andy Gump chin,
   But a purty good gal, for the shape she's in.

I'd like to sing a little song for you tonight; it's called, "Take the Dice Away From Baby, Mother, Before He Craps on the Floor."

Parody of "My Indiana Home"

Once I married a tattooed lady—
It was on one summer's day—
And tattooed upon her body
Was a map of the U.S.A.

And every night before I went to sleep
At her geography I'd take a peek.
Around her neck was Louisiana,
On her hips was Tennessee.
Tattoed upon her back
Was old Hackensack,
In the state of New Jersey.
And just below was old Virginia—
Through those fields I loved to roam.
But when the moon was shining bright upon the Wabash,
I recognized my Indiana home.

Lately my mother-in-law has gotten the dancing craze and upon me devolves the pleasant duty of teaching her some of the latest steps. She weighs 300 pounds—400 on an ice scale—and yet I find it no more difficult to push her around the ballroom floor than if I were moving a piano.

The other night I showed her a new dance, "The Banana Flop." And flop we did—me underneath. I broke three ribs—and a New Year's resolution. My, but she got angry. She said, "I don't know what to call you." I said, "Call me an ambulance."

Last Thursday we all went to a Sunday school picnic. It was held in a beautiful spot called Mosquito Grove. The tickets were $3 each, including the boat ride, admission to the park, and poison oak. A special boat was hired for the occasion. My mother-in-law was the heaviest person on board, so they used her for ballast. There was also a band of music. After every selection they passed around the hat. But after a while some of the passengers got so seasick that they were afraid to risk the hat any more.

After a pleasant sail of two hours—although it didn't seem over seven—our scow finally came in sight of Mosquito Grove. And then came the trouble of landing. The captain was cock-eyed. He looked where he was going. But he didn't go where he was looking. So he ran the front of the scow into the side of the wharf. And it just jarred the passengers so hard that it shook out all my mother-in-law's teeth. I let a little boy pick them up. I was afraid if I stooped down for them myself they might bite me.

THE MONOLOGUE, THE PITCH
AND THE LECTURE

The line that separated a mere assemblage of gag material from a monologue was not always very clear. Nor was the distinction apparently of the least concern to traditional entertainers, who were inclined to label as a monologue almost anything presented by one performer. Indeed, the range of the stock monologue was considerable—from the "stump speeches" and "orations" of minstrelsy to the comedy monologues of chautauqua and vaudeville, the exotic spiels of medicine showmen and carnival barkers, and the full-evening comic lectures so popular in the last half of the nineteenth century. But perhaps it is helpful to see the monologue as a step toward a fully developed sketch: in many cases it was a more or less complete entity, loosely built around some sort of general theme or slight storyline, which could be presented by one entertainer. It is not, of course, that the monologue was without the traditional flexibility found elsewhere in stock material, only that the result was an essentially independent unit designed to be presented within a longer performance.

The first three monologues in this section are classics from the minstrel tradition of the "stump speech"—a topical comic "address," delivered in heavy Negro dialect, and larded with outrageous malapropisms. Frequently used in the Second Part of the show, and sometimes in place of an afterpiece, a stump speech parodied the excesses of the political orator or the black preacher, although a speech included here ("Burlesque Oration on Matrimony") employs the "wench" figure, created by a male minstrel in drag.

In terms of content, a stump speech was often little more than a collection of the sort of standard gags delivered by the endmen, Tambo and Bones, in the First Part of the show. The gags were given a certain unity in the stump speech, however, by the figure of the pompous orator, and by the bizarre imagery and the dazzling free association with which the orator moved from gag to gag.

Two of the stump speeches presented here are taken from amateur minstrel guides. Such guides abounded in the late nineteenth and early twentieth centuries. As the old professional minstrel companies faded away toward the end of the nineteenth century, amateur minstrelsy increased in popularity, because the material was familiar and because the variety format of the show suited the needs of untrained performers. Many of the amateur guides were prepared by professional minstrel men and featured traditional material from their own shows. Thus the guides represented a direct line back to the jokes, scenes and musical material used by the mid-nineteenth century professionals. Besides influencing amateur production, these minstrel guides had a certain currency among later professional entertainers, who transported the old blackface acts to vaudeville, tent shows, burlesque, radio and early motion pictures. Like the gagbooks mentioned in the Introduction and the notes to the previous section, the minstrel guides were inexpensive source books of classic material which could be used "as is" in blackface routines or altered to suit, say, an Irish act. The stump speech was also commonly presented by circus clowns, and Fred Wilson's clown speech is taken from an early broadside sold to spectators at the circus.

Ethnic comedy was a staple of traditional entertainment, and Irish, German (generally referred to as "Dutch") and Jewish acts once were prevalent in vaudeville and other popular forms. Joe Welch may or may not have actually written the ethnic monologue attributed to him here. It could, for example, have been purchased from a professional writer like James Madison—who claimed to originate special material for such major stage figures as Al Jolson, Nora Bayes, and Willie and Eugene Howard, in addition to creating his gagbooks filled with potted jokes and sketches. Or the monologue may simply have been assembled by Welch from bits and pieces culled from gagbooks, minstrel guides, and other people's routines. It is very likely that this is the case, and that Welch is more *auteur*, as the word is used to describe some modern film directors, than actual "author" of the little monologue, which doubtless went through dozens of variations on stage before its creator had shaped the material just as he wanted it.

Welch's monologue "Troubles" is a piece of so-called "Hebrew comedy," to use the phrase of the day, with strong connections to the "Dutch" tradition. The framework holding the gags together is a slender one—a recitation of the speaker's multifarious troubles. Among them is a variation of the ancient "fly in the soup" gag.

Francis Wilson was a well-known performer in musical comedy, revue and vaudeville. The monologue bearing his name, which is more tightly organized than the one attributed to Welch, centers around the trials of a dentist's office. (Dentist and doctor routines were staples of virtually every form of popular entertainment: elsewhere in this volume, for example, are the famous "Over the River, Charlie," a traditional medicine show sketch, and a well-known burlesque bit, "Prickly Heat.") Wilson's monologue illustrates the flexibility of many popular acts. Much of the monologue is actually a dialogue between

Wilson and a dental assistant and, later, between Wilson and the dentist. In fact, these sections virtually make up a brief "bit" with Wilson playing all the roles.

Recitations in rhyme were common in many forms of entertainment. Johnny Patterson's sentimental "Only a Clown" has its origin in the circus. The *Hamlet* burlesque may also have a circus origin, but it is typical of the sort of material used in many popular shows. The "Old Fashioned Girl," another rhymed recitation, was collected from Anna Blair Miller, who performed it in traveling tent chautauqua for many years. Traveling chautauqua, an important form of entertainment in rural areas from the turn of the century until about 1930, featured a unique blend of oratory, musical material, and spotlessly laundered vaudeville. Miller's "Old Fashioned Girl" combined both verse and snatches of popular song in a recitation typical of the sort of genteel comedy favored on the chautauqua circuits.

Lois Madden's version of "A Deck of Cards," which she performed in tent shows and other types of entertainment, is interesting in several respects. This immensely popular monologue, which also appears in a later section as a minstrel dialogue, tells a complete story, and a serious if somewhat sentimentalized one. In later years it was frequently recorded, perhaps most effectively by comedian and singer Phil Harris. Mrs. Madden's version has an untypical Italian village setting suggested to her by her husband's wartime experiences.

The tradition of the popular lecture was important in a number of forms of entertainment. The dime museum, the panorama, and the carnival and circus side shows, for example, all employed lecturers or "inside talkers" who explained the exhibits with appropriate oratorical flourishes. Some also used "outside talkers," whose job it was to draw audiences into the show with a "pitch" or "grind" performed repeatedly outside the tent or theatre. Another brand of talker or "pitchman" worked the medicine shows, peddling remedies to audiences between the acts at free evenings of vaudeville.

The three pitches included here were collected from Fred Bloodgood ("Doc" Foster), a master lecturer who worked as both a carnival and medicine show pitchman. Two of Bloodgood's three brief lectures were designed to sell medicine and candy, a staple on most medicine shows and tent rep shows; the third was used to draw audiences into a carnival "geek show," a somewhat lurid exhibition featuring a freak who ate broken glass, razor blades or live birds and reptiles. Although Bloodgood's lectures seem quaint and tongue-in-cheek today, they were originally presented in a serious way and were taken quite seriously by spectators.

The full-evening lecture was a great nineteenth-century institution, and many prominent figures from the literary, political, scientific, and theatrical worlds toured extensively with talks and readings. Humorists were especially popular on the lecture circuit, among them, of course, Mark Twain. Twain's contemporary Josh Billings (Henry Wheeler Shaw) is virtually forgotten today; in the second half of the nineteenth century, however, his rough but pithy comic writing was widely read and his lectures well attended. This section ends with an extended lecture by Billings, filled with amazing transitions and containing an ironic set of rules for local lecture committee which must have endeared him to the other professional talkers of his day.

ORANGES. A STUMP SPEECH.

Ladies and Gentlemen; The speech which I am about to deliver has been delivered with marked success at most of the funerals in the country, and as a tear-provoker is equaled only by the sweet-scented and savory onion.

I, myself, have spoken it with more or less success, principally less, in all cities and towns of Europe, Asia and Hoboken—where I have spoken it.

The last place where I got it off was in Rome—New York. It pleased the audience very much, and the leading citizens determined to assist in my triumphal entry out of the town.

At first they thought of carrying me out in a gilded chariot drawn by prancing Arab steeds, but the chariot not being available, they substituted a rail!

But I must not digress. G. W. Childs, A. M., remarks in the "Rise and Fall of the Roman Umpires," that the man who digresses is lost—and it takes a liberal reward to find him again! Therefore, I will at once continue with my subject, Oranges.

Oranges, my friends, is a sweet subject; it is a juicy subject, and like women, ladies and gentlemen, is something which we never get enough of.

In a general way, I mean, my hearers. I myself have enough of lovely woman—my wife weighs three hundred and fifty with her stockings off. She is here to listen to me this evening, as her father has just died, and she wishes to get in a suitable frame of mind to attend his send off.

Speaking of funerals; funerals are not what they used to be. In the good old times we used to slam the corpse in a pine box and bury him gently. But now, brethren, no man, be he ever so humble, dies without wanting gilt-edged obsequies (obsequies is a good word, fellow bull-dozers, and I am proud of it. It took me a day or two to find out what it meant, as at first I thought that it was some new kind of baking powder). Baking powders, gentlemen, should be used with care, as, like the thermometer, they are bound to rise.

My youngest son, a sweet child with deep blue eyes, and a head like a burning prairie, swallowed a baking powder yesterday.

He immediately became an Inflationist, and looked as if he had lived on a luxurious diet of dried apples and hot water for a week.

We loved that boy, my wife and I did, but we could not keep him. He inflated until he had to take his meals out of doors, and sleep in Central Park. Every time that he appeared in public the police would arrest him for blocking up the street. So we had to tie a red string around his neck and sell him to an ary nut [aeronaut] for a balloon. And as a balloon he made a decided success.

Success, my friends, has a good many different meanings. For example: The other day an estimable female relative of my wife's mother attempted to light the fire with kerosene. The fire did light, that was a success, but where, oh, where was the lovely lightist? Dispersed over ten square acres, and the only thing that we found intact was her tongue. That was still a-wagging.

But, my dear hearers, I will not detain you longer—the authorities will not allow me to. Therefore, I bid you all a good evening, and hope that you have learned all you want to know about oranges.

BURLESQUE ORATION ON MATRIMONY. DELIVERED IN THE CHARACTER OF AUNTY CHLOEY.

Human Critters, Hemale Humbugs, an' Female Wictims.—Straighten up, and listen to ole Aunty Chloey, while she splainties de question of matrimony.

Matrimony am a humbug, husbands am tyrants, love am a sham, an' domestic bliss am a dam suck in.

In de fust place, dar's de honeymoon, or in some cases de winegar moon, dat passes away like the contents of a clam chowder pot afore a parcel of hungry niggers. Den, aha!—den, den you may wear your weddin'-dress at de wash-tub, an' your seventeen-penny calico on Sundays, an' your lord an' master won't know it. You may pick up your own pocket hankerfitch, an' rip your dress up de back, stretchin' across de table for anoder flapjack, an' he don't boder to help you!—eh? ah? How's dat?

An' all de time he is layin' his breakfast in, just as if it was de last meal he was a gwine to eat on dis side of de kingdom comin'. Den he gets up from de table, lights his cigar wid de last evening's paper, afore you've had a chance to read it—gives three or four whiffs at it, just enough to set your head achin' all day—eh? ah? How is dat?

Den, jist as he's goin' out, you ax him if he won't do a little errand for you. What does he say—eh? ah? Why, he tells you dat he's very sorry he can't oblige you, but he's so pressed wid business. Dat's de 'scuse. You needn't grin at me, you he-crocodiles! you know it's de trufe—eh? ah? how is dat?

But s'pose you was to see him about 'leven o'clock, takin' ice-cream wid a young lady in Delmonico's, while de misfortunate wife is at home, puttin' new linin's to his coat-sleeves, or sewin' buttons on his what-you-may-call-'em—eh? ah? how is dat?

Den, when he comes home at night, he'll just walk in, pull off his overcoat, and say, "How de do, Sally?" or somethin' just as cool—blow up de chillum—may be wallup dem—an' down he'll sit in front of de stove, pull de newspaper put ob his pocket, and read it all to hisself. He eats his supper, and down he lies on de sophia, and snores away till nine o'clock. Den he gets up, and says he'll take a walk for half an hour—mind you, de sarpint don't ax his poor wife to come along—away he goes, and you doesn't see him again till two o'clock in de mornin'—eh? ah? how is dat?

Nex' mornin' you ax him to let you have a little money. What's de consequence? Why, he heaved a sigh like a kipoodle pup dyin' wid de toofache, an' axes you won't fifty cents do, as money is very scarce jist now; jist as if you was gwine to get shoes, stockings, pettiskirts, flannens, and free-cornered hankerficher for de young ones, for half a dollar! Dam nonsense—eh? ah? how is dat?

Gals, wenches, an' oder shemales, take my advice; set you affections on cats, dogs, parrots, ginny-goats, bull-frogs, or canary-birds—but let matrimony alone. It's a swindle, a humbug, a suck-in; in de-gumphatic lanwidge of Mrs. Stanton, it's a dead beat. Tink of it—carryin' eight or ten ot fourteen or twenty-one chillum frough de meazles, and de mumps, and de hoopin' cough, and de rash, and de itch, an' scratch-gravel, and all de oder complaints, some of 'em free or four times over! golly, it's enough to set dis ole wench crazy to tink along about it—eh? ah? how is dat?

Den you may squeeze, an' save, an' twist, an' turn, an' dig, an' delve, an' den you die! Den, of course, your husband goes and gits married agin, and takes what you have saved to dress his second wife wid; and she'll take your lileness to make a fireboard—eh? ah? how is dat?

But what's de use of wastin' my precious breff wid all my talkin'? All you gals will go an' try it, de very fust chance you git. Dar's a sort of hyferlutin' about the lovyers you can't resist let ole Aunty Chloey spoke as she will. I do believe one half o' de world am idiots, and de oder half fools—eh? ah? how is dat?

HOW ADAM AND EVE TURNED WHITE. A DARKEY'S SERMON TO HIS CONGREGATION.

My beloved sistern and breddering. I'm a man what reads a great deal, and I'm going to 'splain to you how Adam and Eve turned white, for dey was originally black as you am, or I am. Well, it 'pears dat de Lawd, after he done made Adam and Eve, sot 'em in de Garden ob Edem, dat de Lawd he tol' 'em bofe dat dar was a sartin tree dar and dat dey musn't eat none of eet's fruit. Dis tree, it 'pears to me, if I don't disremember, eet bared a kind 'er apple. You know same as me, dat a woman's a powerful curus pusson. She allus like to be a-peekin' and a pryin' into something or other—no matter whether it consarns her or not. Ole Miss Eve—dat dar was ole man Adam's wife—she warnt to be stopped from nothin'. 'Twant long afore she knowed dat de Lawd didn't want her to meddle wif dem apples dat she went and made a pie and sort er bobbecued some of the Lawd's apples. She did this, for truth. 'Twant no yarn dat some of de mean white folks have brung agin ole Miss Eve. She sartinly did get de Lawd's apples. When dat ole woman don got 'em, sure enough, de Lawd he war monstrous mad. He put all de blame on ole Adam, 'cause de Lawd he sorter think dat ole man Adam oughter have took better care of ole Miss Eve dan to 'low her to bobbecue de Lawd's apples. When de pair of 'em had done eat de apples dey crope off and hid in de bushes. Dey war so scared of de Lawd, dat scared ain't no name for de business. Dey war so scared dat dey turned deef and den dey turned white. Dey neber did zactly git over their scare. Dey did git to hearin' ag'in, but their skins never did get colored no more, and dat am how de white man come here. He's white because of de meanness of ole man Adam and ole Miss Eve. But let me go on wif my history. When de Lawd done found out dat dese ole pussons had done eat some of his apples, he war monstrous mad. He yell out: "Yo' Adam!" but 'pears Mr. Adam he didn't hear. Den de Lawd ses, ses he: "Adam, why yo' eat my apples, sah? Is you so deef you can't hear nuffin', or is you gone foolish, sah? You go right away and bring Miss Eve here, sah; gyarments or no gyarments!"

My friends, you mought say dat ar war powerful bad manners of de Lawd. But den de Lawd ain't agawine to be fooled with. When He's plum mad he don't spar' no one. Bime-by up crope ole Miss Eve walkin' sorter behind ole man Adam, and kind of giggling and peeking over de ole man's shoulder. When dey done come up to de Lawd, de Lawd he ses, ses he: "You's both a par of no count triflin niggers. You done stole my apples, and you's fixin' to git my chickens next. Git outer dis garden bofe of you, and never come back here no more for nuthin', not even for your gyarments. Git out from here quick." Den de Lawd showed 'em de gate, and give de ole debil de job ter watch dat gate, to see dat neider Miss Eve nor Mr. Adam come in dar no more. And Miss Eve, she was forced to sit in de bushes outside dat gate, 't'well Mr. Adam, he done made 'em some new gyarments. And while Mr. Adam, he sewed, Miss Eve she sang dat good ole hymn: "I Loves to steal awhile."

And dat, my friends, am de trufe of de trouble what ole man Adam had wif de Lawd, and de history of how de white man come here. Bofe Miss Eve and Mr. Adam dey war so scared dat dey never got back their color no more. Some of their young'uns war black and some war white, most same as you often see an ole white hen with a hull gang of chickens, some white and some black. Don't fool with de Lawd, my friends, else he'll scare you so bad dat you'll be arunnin' around looking foolish, jest same as de mean white trash.

STUMP SPEECH
BY THE KING OF JESTERS, FRED WILSON
CLOWN TO BUCKLEY & CO.'S NATIONAL CIRCUS

Fellow citizens—Unexpectedly called upon to address you, I cannot find words in etiquet to express myself on this momentous occasion, but like all other political aspirants, I will confine my few remarks to matters and things that affects this our great and glorious country, America. It is bounded on the north by the aurora borealis, on the east by the rising sun and lumber yards, on the west by the ocean, and on the south as far as you like to go. We have the broadest lakes, the longest rivers, the swiftest steam boats, the tallest shanghais, more mud and rain, and the handsomest galls in all creation! But fellow citizens, we have got a great country, we are agoing to have it fenced in as soon as we can get help enough to split the rails. Why this town, in my recollection, was a silent desolation and a howling wilderness; here the diabolical Indian reigned supreme and wild cats built their solitary nests, and where we are now congregated together the prairie wolf used the gallop along with his majestic tail behind him. But, fellow citizens, a change has come over us; instead of stragling wig wams, you behold piles of bricks and mortar, and that great piece of public enterprise and spirit, the jail, now stands where the peblecan used to scream in the wilderness, and around our subborbs you can see the flourishing potater hill and melodious pig-sty, and where quietly goes to grass the statley goose and majestic gander. Fellow citizens, in view of the rise and progress of our country, I now nominate myself before this convention as a candidate for next president. I am an independent candidate in an independent state, dependent on an independent people. I am opposed to monopoly, cholera, and bad liquors. I am in favor of equality, union and good brandy and sugar. I go in for the union because the ladies do,— they do say that the ladies are in for the union to a man. Some of the fanatics of the north and hotspurs of the south talk of dissolving us; they may as well try to skull up Niagara falls in a pot-ash kettle with a crow bar for an oar. If I am elected I intend to abolish flogging in the navy, and introduce it into congress. As for the banks I am down on them; a fellow passed a bad bill on me the other day, it was of the government stock bank, of Annarboar, Michigan; it was like a rum shop to me. I could not pass it. In regard to the Maine liquor law I am so dry I can hardly speak on that important subject. Rum ruined a big brother of mine and when I see a bottle of it I want to clutch it by the neck so as to get satisfaction out of it. They have the Maine liquor law in Indiana but they are agoing to have a provision put in that bill allowing every man to drink a little when they wash sheep, every man is agoing to get a sheep and wash it, then Indiana will be celebrated for clean wool. But I don't believe in washing sheep too much. I saw a man the other day and I thought he had been washing a whole flock he was dead drunk laying in the mud by the side of a hog. The hog had a ring in his snout, the man had one on his finger. I screamed, we are known by the company we keep,—the hog gave a grunt, got up and left, ashamed of his company.

Now if you will elect me president, I will pass a law that our lakes, creeks and rivers shall run full of rum, gin, brandy and sugar. I'll make the tetotal party pay for it. Oh, if I'm President there shall be no orphan children in the country—I'll gather them all. There shall be no widows—I'll marry them all. I'll have the walls of our country made of mush and milk, so that the poor may eat and grow fat! So cheer up, the country's safe!

Songs and speeches of the Clown can be had at the stand.

TROUBLES BY JOE WELCH

Maybe you think I'm happy. I got the bad luck. I join me last vinter a lodge. I get seven dollars a veek ven I'm sick an' I can't get sick! The only thing I ever get me is dyspepski. I drank a pussy-cat cafe. The doctor came in my house and say I shall get him a baper and pencil to write de prescription. I couldn't find the baper and bencil but I find a piece of chalk. He say, "Nefer mind. I write it on de door an' ven you find the baper and bencil you shall copy it." He told me I shall bring it to the drugstore an' get de prescription. I give him a dollar an' he say good-by. I don't read nor write. I shall not expose my ignorance. So I get the screwdriver and take the door off and bring it to the drugstore and tell the druggist he shall give me for five cents the prescription. Shure!

Today I saw a ole voman, sixty years of age, jump right in front of a car. I give her a pull and save her life, and she says I'm a hobo. Oh, how she thank me. She say, "I'll take you home with me," and I valk on de street mit her. Eferybody laugh. Dey think I got de mash. Ven ve get to her house she set me down in de parlor and she say, "I introduce you to my son-in-law, Mister Villiams." Und she say, "Mister Villiams, dis is Mister Jacobson. He safe me my life today from gettin' killed by the car." He look at me all ofer an' he say, "Oh, is that so?" Then he say, "Are you the fellow what save my mother-in-law?" I say, "Yes, sir." So he say, "Come into the front room. I vant to haf a talk mit you." I vill nefer safe anoder life!

De oder day I vent to de Grand Central depot and I lay me a fife-dollar bill on the shelf and say, "I vant a ticket for Yonkers." He say, "Excursion?" I say, "No, funeral." Ven I got to Yonkers, I vent to de cemetery to visit my brother's dead grave. I kneel down on de grave and I pray and cry for two hours. Den I look at de names on de grave and I see me de mistake. I was crying two hours for nothing. When I find de right grave I shall cry all over again. I vent to de janitor of de cemetery and I ask him, "Vere is my brother buried?'' He say, ''How long has he been dead?'' I say, ''Six months.'' He say, ''Vat is his name?'' I say, ''Nathan Jacobson.'' He say, ''Vat did he look like?'' I say, ''He is de picture of me.'' He say, ''Impossible! Anybody that looks like you ought to be dead longer than six months.''

I live no more vid my wife. She got jealousness. She make me I shall give her money efery veek. I vell remember ven ve got married. I vore a stovepipe hat, and a white shirt and collar—clean. My vife vore a taffy silk skirt an' a vaist. All openwork. You can look inside. Here is a piece of lace, here is a hole. Here is another piece of lace. Then you vait a minute. Here is two holes.

De oder night I vent to see ''Ten Nights in a Bathtub.'' It's a sensationals play like ''Saphy.'' Only nobody gets carried up de stairs. But a feller gets kicked down the stairs. Vell, a pistol shot makes de baby cry and de usher gomes down and says, ''If dat baby cries again, go outside und get your money back.'' De next night ve go to anoder play, und I say, ''Rachel, do you like de play?'' She say, ''No, that's a humbug.'' I say, ''Stick a pin in de baby.''

Vell, von night I go to the theatre und I get a seat on a ladder, and two fellers comes on de stage and shake hands. I dink dey is good friends. Pretty soon dey begin to fight und for nothing. Some feller calls out, ''Punch him in de breadbasket.'' Another feller say, ''Hit him in de uppercuts.'' I holler out, ''Hit him in de kishkers.'' A feller who sat next to me got excited and kicked me. He asked me who I dink shall vin de fight. I tell him I don't know and ask him who it is. He says, ''Why, Terry McGovern. He'll knock his roof off, and if he don't I'll knock yours off.'' He say, ''I bet you two dollars to one that McGovern wins.'' I say, ''No.'' He say, ''I'll bet you five dollars to one.'' I say, ''No.'' He say, ''I'll bet you fifty dollars you don't know you're alive.'' I vas afraid to bet.

Vell, I came out of de theatre and I vent into a beer saloon on de corner and I laid a twenty-five-cent piece on de counter and I say, ''Give me a nice large glass of beer. I got dry in de neck.'' I vait for de change an' I no get him. I dink dis must be a high-toney place. Den I say to de bartender, ''Didn't you forget something?'' He said, ''Yas, I forgot more than you ever knew.'' I say, ''I gif you a quarter.'' He say, ''You gave me a nickel.'' I say, ''You're a liar!'' Oh-oh! The minute I say, ''You're a iar,'' I got such uppercuts. I vent out to de street an' see a big feller standin' on de corner. I say to him, ''Do you vant to make a dollar—cash?'' He says, ''It's a pipe.'' I say, ''Come in de saloon and punch a man in de eye.'' He says, ''All right.'' So I give him right avay in his hand de dollar and I bring him in de saloon. He says, ''Vere is he?'' I showed him the bartender, and the big feller says, ''Did you hit him?'' He says, ''Yes, an' I'll hit him again.'' An' he kept his word. De big feller says, ''I'll dare you to hit him once more.'' I vished he hadn't dared him. Vell, vat do you think de big feller says? He says, ''Come on, don't spend another nickel in the joint.''

The other day I got me arrested and I vent to de jail in de Black Maria. Von feller in the carriage says to another feller, "Hello there, Cockeye Mulligan! How long you got dis time?" "Vell," Cockeye says, "two years an' six months." "For why?" says the feller. "For nothin'," says Cockeye. "De judge ees a stiff." I say to Cockeye, "For nothing you get two years an' six months?" He says, "Yes, I stuck a knife in a dago's heart."

Another feller says, "Hello there, Jimmy! Gimme a cigar." Jimmy says, "All I got is a butt." He says, "Sing it over 'till I get a vhiff." The feller vat set next to me in the carriage was cryin'. I says to him, "Vat are you cryin' fer?" He says, "Don't bother me or I'll knock your block off." I says, "How much did you get?" He says, "I got ten years." I says, "For nothin' too?" He says, "No, I tapped a guy on the nut with a sandbag and took his clock." Den he says, "Did you ever get a tap on the nut?" I says, "No." He says, "Vell, keep on chewin' de rag to me an' you'll get it."

He says next, "How long did you get?" I says, "Ten days." He says, "Vat are you kickin' about? That's sleepin' time." Ven ve got to de jail de keeper says to me, "What are you here for—bigamy?" He knows I'm a nice-lookin' feller. He takes me in his private office, and he takes in his hand a pen, and he has a book to write in, an' he says, "What's your name?" I think to myself, I vill nefer tell him my name in a hundred years. He says, "Answer quick! What's your name?" I says, "Isaac Fitzpatricks." He says, "Say, you're a fresh mug. Don't make any funny cracks around here or I'll sink one of your lamps." One of the fellers whispered to me, "He's all right. He's a good feller but you want to tell him he's daffy." So I says, "You're daffy." "Oh," he says, "I am, am I?" Vell, ten minutes later I voke up.

De other day I thought I could take a Turkish bath, but the man was going to charge me a dollar. I said, "That's too much." So he said, "I'll send you twelve tickets for ten dollars." I said, "Vat do you take me for? How do I know I'm going to live twelve years more."

The other day my friend Rosenski took his boy in a restaurant to get a bowl of soup. Jakey commenced to eat, an' he grabbed his father's arm an' says, "Papa, there's a fly in der soup." Rosenski says, "Eat der soup an' vait till you come down to der fly. Den tell de vaiter and he'll give you another bowl for nothing."

FRANCIS WILSON'S THRILLING WRESTLING ACT WITH A WILD DENTIST

"I have been to the dentist and had a tooth pulled," began Francis Wilson, the lively little comedian, with his usual effervescent geniality, "and now I can sympathize with gamblers who have had big joints pulled."

"My friends said it was a shame to have a bad tooth in such a good mouth; and, though I wanted to keep it a secret, it's out at last.

"The dentist I went to had pulled teeth from all the crowned heads of Europe, and he ws so feminine in his manners that he drew my attention a few days before. He was good at bridge work, having labored on the Brooklyn Bridge as an engineer before taking up dentistry.

"Everybody liked him, he said, and he had pulled the teeth of a whole family, including a few garden rakes and a saw. To put costly caps on teeth was his crowning glory. And yet his personal appearance would not betoken any greatness.

"He had an abnormal head, which was entirely hairless; and, as I viewed his bald pate, I thought that if he was a self-made man he must have made his head with the hair side inside to keep his thoughts warm.

"I stood with diffidence before the entrance to the office. On one door was a sign reading 'Pull,' and that seemed to add more horrors to the grim situation.

"I did not care to enter such a grewsome place alone, so I waited until I was beside myself with fear, and then I went in. Getting inside the door, I was approached by a young lady with spectacular hair, who asked what she could do for me.

"In my nervous state I asked her to come closer and I would whisper it to her, fearing that the dentist himself might overhear me and pounce upon me without a moment's notice.

"The young lady looked at me in a bewildered manner, and then shouted, quite flippantly, I thought:

" 'You've got a nerve!'

" 'Ye-e-es,' I stammered, 'that's it. It's exposed, too, and I want it killed, electrocuted, garroted or poisoned—it is wearing my life away.'

"She opened a door marked 'Private' and bid me enter. I, like the martyr that I was, reluctantly walked in. There was a large chair in the center of the room that seemed to be stretching out its big arms for me, eager to grapple with my carcass, while all the sets of teeth lying about the place seemed to be snapping at me, anxious to get a bite of my plump anatomy. The decorations in the room were all true to life, except the teeth—they were false.

"The chief puller-out (down on the sidewalk the dental company had a puller-in) arose as I entered and begged of me to take a seat. This surprised me for a minute. I was not used to having seats offered to me, having traveled on the crowded 'L' trains for many years.

"At last, however, I climbed into the chair and mumbled, absent-mindedly:

" 'Don't shave too close, please, and try not to stop up my nostrils with sour lather and lead me to believe I am suffering with hay fever, while, at the same time, you are endeavoring to gouge my eye out with a brush that is sadly in need of a wig, and—'

"But I was suddenly brought to my senses when the dentist jerked back my head as though it was a brake handle, and yanked open my mouth so that he could get a peep into its vast depths.

"He held tightly onto my chin and forehead. Afraid he'd fall in, I suppose. Then he took up a tack puller with a mirror attachment on the end and commenced to search my mouth for something. I thought maybe he had dropped his hat in, or perhaps he wanted to see where all my choice language came from.

" 'Which one is it?' he asked.

" 'That white one,' I replied, pointing towards the interior of my mouth.

" 'Has it got a cavity in it?' he asked again.

" 'No,' I retorted, making a play at levity. 'It's got a clove, parts of three meals and a bunch of toothpicks in it.'

" 'Ah!' he shouted, jubilantly, after a further search, 'I have the acher.'

" 'Well, well!' I gurgled, smilingly, 'I wanted the earth; but all I got was an acher. Can't you fill it?'

" 'Indeed no,' he giggled. 'I'm too small to fill such a big opening.'

"Then he asked whether I wanted it pulled by gas. I told him it made no difference to me; I didn't care whether it was abstracted by gas or in the dark.

" 'I have gas, cocaine and other preparations,' he said, 'and I can give you whatever extract you want.'

" 'All right,' I replied; 'if it's all the same to you, I'll take some vanilla extract; it doesn't leave such a bad taste in the mouth.'

"He only smiled; and, after fussing around a while, he placed a rubber d-m in my mouth and tried to see how far he could stretch my jawbones without snapping them in two.

"Then he wheeled a tank over toward the chair and asked if I had ever taken gas before. I told him no, because I never did care much for light lunches; and then I asked him if gas hadn't gone up this year.

" 'No,' he replied, jerkily; 'but some of it will go down in a few minutes.'

"I told him the only way I thought I could take gas with a little brandy in it. And, as I viewed the tank, it reminded me so much of an old flame of mine whom I had turned down.

"Before he administered the gas he put his ear to my chest and said:

" 'Your heart doesn't beat so perfectly.'

" 'I know it,' I answered. 'It loses about twelve ticks a day; but next summer I'm going to have it stop for a while so that I can get it cleaned up a bit.'

" 'Have you ever had a torpid liver?' he inquired, after a pause.

"I understood him to ask if I had ever had a torpid liver, and I replied:

" 'No; but I've had shooting pains up my back. But,' I added, 'you're not going to pull my heart and liver, too?'

"He made no reply, but lifted a gas tube with some mouthpiece on the end of it; and, after he had me muzzled, he told me to take a deep breath. I did so, but shoved the tube away very quickly.

" 'I can't get any air with that thing on my face.'

"He told me to try again, and I did so. After that I lost my conscience. I don't know where I lost it, though, and it's so hard to find such small things.

"When I came to my toothache was gone. So was my watch. So was the dentist. But that individual returned in a few minutes drying his hands. He had evidently put my jewelry in soak. When I asked him for the missing valuables he only laughed. Said the gas made some people do very queer things. I thought so, too.

"When I climbed down from the chair I handed the dentist fifteen cents and looked around for a whisk broom to dust off my hat. But after the bald-pated gentleman stared at me as though I was a private burlesque show, I remembered, quite suddenly, that I wasn't in a barber shop.

"As I left the place I felt relieved—of two dollars and several other things.

"And, would you believe it, my corns haven't ached since, and I'm thinking that they were the roots of that tooth.

"I am longing for the time when nature will provide me with a false set of teeth. Then when one of them aches I can leave it with a toothsmith on my way downtown and call for it in the evening."

ONLY A CLOWN
AS RECITED BY JOHHNY PATTERSON

Yes, thanks, sir, I'll have a small measure of beer, though I don't often treat
    myself so;
I'm "Only a Clown" with no kindred or friends, no life but that in the show;
My heaven—the canvas that covers our ring, and shields us from rains and
    from heats.
My horizon—all that I have ever known, ends with the last row of seats.

I was once not alone as you see me to-day, I'd a mate in my "Act on the Bar."
My wife she's an angel in heaven I know—on earth she was always a star.
How did she die? No every day death; I'll tell you—but first let me pause—
She died of a shock she got in the ring—and I myself was the cause.

'Twas a benefit night, about five years ago; the tent stood in this very place,
Every seat had been sold the morning before, the people had come from a
    race;
We had a dangerous "Act on the Bar," but we all got a small extra fee.
Our turn was the next, we stood at the gate; Cordello, Polly and me.

I feared this Cordello, a man in our troupe, with his piercing and wicked black
    eyes.

And he hated me with all of his heart, as I'd stolen away his great prize:
For he'd often asked Polly to come be his wife, but no answer from her could
  he get.
And I've known him to swear by all that was good, that he "would be square
  with me yet."

The net it was this—a bar hung on high some fifty-five feet from the ground.
Cordello would hang, and Polly and I were to spring in his hands with a
  bound;
A dangerous trick, as you'll see at a glance, and one that depends all in all,
On the man that's above, for were he inclined, he could let either one of us
  fall.

We sprung into the ring amid the applause, seemingly pleased for the while,
But my heart it beat fast, and I shook like a leaf, for I read that dark man's
  wicked smile;
Then we each took our place for this leap into death! Cordello was quickly on
  high,
But his lips seemed to say as he went up the rope, "our time's come; it's now
  you or I."

He had fixed himself firm and swung by his knees, the music was braying out
  loud,
My wife posed herself to spring to his arms, or else dash headlong in the
  crowd.
The signal was given—one bound did she make—thank God her arms tight
  round his neck.
Now 'twas for me to trust my life there, or else fall below a poor wreck.

He stretched out his hands, but it seemed just the same as the devil, who
  always cries "come;"
His eyes they stared wild, I then saw the truth, the man was half crazy with
  rum,
My eyesight was dim, all seemed in a blur, in a second away I would be,
When my wife swung around and hung by the bar and cried loudly, "Ben
  jump to me."

It was there that I jumped, and was safe in her arms before half a second could
  pass;
Cordello was swung from the bar by the shock to the ring far below, a mere
  mass.
But Polly grew worse from that very night, she so gallantly saved my poor
  life—
And that's why you see me, sir, "Only a Clown," no money, no friends and

no wife.

HAMLET

Last night the boss slips me a ticket
  For one of them opera shows.
An' the name of the show is called "Hamlet",
  So I digs up my glad rags and goes.
Well, it's gloom from the minute it opens
  'Till the time the theayter shuts,
An' the company's half of them looney
  An' the rest of the cast is plain nuts.
The tenor's a goof known as Hamlet
  But really his name should be Gloom.
He's a regular "Life O' the party, e' is
  As jolly and gay as a tomb,
His old man was King o' the Denmarks,
  But the poor guy's gone weak in the bean.
For his old man 'as been croaked by his uncle
  Who then ups and marries the Queen.
So young Hamlet hangs round kinda sad like
  An' he talks to himself like a nut
For as yet he ain't hep that his father
  Was bumpted off by his uncle—the Mutt,
One night he slips out o' the castle
  An' goes up on the roof for some air,
When along comes the ghost of his father
  An' he shoots him an earful for fair.
"Dot lowlife, your uncle, has croaked me,
  An' 'e's went off an' married yer ma.
Will you let that rat hand you the double?"
  Sez Hamlet "Now you match me, Pa."

Young Ham has a frail called Ophelia,
  An' her pa is a dreary old goof,
And they can't dope why Hamlet's gone batty
  They don't know what he saw on the roof,
Well, Ham goes an' calls on his mother,
  An' he bawls out the old girl for fair.
Then he sees somethin' move in the curtains;
  An' he thinks that the uncle is there.
So he jabs with his sword through the curtain
  An' he cries, "Now we're even, by gad!"

But it isn't the King—it's Polonius,
  An' he's killed poor Ophelia's old dad.

Then Ophelia, poor kid, just goes daffy
  When she hears how her old man is crowned.
And she walks around singin' like crazy,
  'Till she falls in the lake and gets drowned.
There's a jolly old scene in the graveyard
  Where Prince Hamlet gets into a scrap
With Ophelia's big brother Laertes,
  Who wants to puss up Hamlet's nap.
Then the King says "Now, boys, don't act nasty,
  I know how to fight this thing out,
I've got some tin swords at the castle
  And We'll frame up a nice friendly bout."
Then he winks at Laertes an' whispers;
  "We'll knock this here nut for a goal
I'll smear up your sword with some poison.
  An' we'll make this Hamlet look like a fool."

So they pull off the bout like they planned it,
  But the King thinks his scheme may slip up,
So he orders a cold drink for Hamlet,
  An' some poison he sneaks in the cup!
Then Ham and Laertes start fighting
  An' the King slips Laertes the wink,
But the Queen, she ain't wise to what's doin',
  An' she swallows the King's poison drink.
Then Hamlet gets stabbed in the shoulder
  And he sees 'ow 'es framed from the start,
So he switches the swords on Laertes
  An' stabs the poor bum through the heart.
Then he runs the sword right through his uncle.
  An' he says, "Well, let's call it a day."
Then de Queen dies, then de King dies, then Laertes dies,
      an' Hamlet dies.
  I think it's a heleva play.

OLD-FASHIONED GIRL

[Sung]
It was an old fashioned garden,
Just an old fashioned garden.

But it carried me back, to that dear little shack
In the land of long ago.

I saw an old fashioned missus,
Getting old fashioned kisses
In that old fashioned garden,
From an old fashioned beau.

[*Spoken*]
It seems so strange that grandma, some 50 years ago,
Upon returning from a dance, or party, don't you know.
When at the gate each laddy bid adieu to each fair maid.
On leaving, he would surely sing a good-night serenade.
Now on occasions like this you would hear
A song, which now-a-days would sound quite queer:

[*Sung*]
Good night, Ladies.
Good night, Ladies.
Good night, Ladies.
We're going to leave you now.

[*Spoken*]
What a difference, now-a-days, you really can't deny
The fact that songs have changed a lot from days that have gone by.
Of course, you know, this sort of thing is now quite out of date,
And on those sweet occasions, here's the song I heard of late:

[*Sung*]
Yes, sir, that's my baby.
No, sir, I don't mean maybe.
Yes, sir, that's my baby now.

[*Spoken*]
But things like this could not occur when grandma was a girl.
Now, the streetcars that they used to have, when grandmama was a girl
Are different from those we have in this time's busy whirl.
A polite conductor on our streetcar would be something new.
Conductors in the olden days were too good to be true.
When grandmama was a girl, it was a fact,
That this is how conductors used to act:

"The next stop is Times' Square, change cars for City Hall.
Be careful, don't soil your skirt on that dirty step.

Oh, here's a lovely seat. Are you quite comfortable?
Will you have a transfer?
Have I your permission to start the car?''
Ding. Ding.

What a difference now-a-days. You really can't deny
The fact that things have changed a lot from days that have gone by
Now-a-days, whenever you desire to catch a car,
This kind of treatment you will get, no matter who you are:

"Watch the step.
No, no transfer.
Hurry up, step lively
Look out there, you wanna break your neck.
Ding. Ding.

But things like this could not occur when grandma was a girl.

A DECK OF CARDS

Ladies and Gentlemen—with your kind permission, I should like to repeat to you a little story that was told me the other day. This is no reflection on any particular denomination, and is not derogatory in the least. During this recent great war of ours, up on the Tyrrhenian coast of Italy, a company of U. S. soldiers was marching through a little village. It was early in the morning and the soldiers were very tired. Now in the center of the village stood the church. The peasants were slowly gathering for their morning worship. The captain of our boys was notified and asked that, if they cared to, they were more than welcome to attend the service. Whereupon our boys filed slowly into the church, become seated, and the service proceeded. It was noted by the captain that one of his men was displaying a deck of playing cards. After the services were concluded, the boy was brought before his commanding officer to give an account of why he displayed a deck of playing cards in a house of the Lord. When the boy was brought before his commanding officer, he tried to explain to him in this manner:

"Sir, I meant no harm. You see, whenever I look at the ace, or the one-spot, it tells me there is but one God, God Almighty. And when I look at the deuce, or the two-spot, I think of the Father and the Son; and when I look at the trey, or the three-spot, I think of the three great wise men who followed the star into Bethlehem. And when I look at the four-spot, I think of the four great apostles, Matthew, Mark, Luke, and John. And when I look at the five-spot, I think of the five foolish virgins who ruined their names, three repented and were saved, two were foolish and turned back. And when I look at the six-spot, it tells me that my Lord created the heavens and earth in just six days. And when I look at the seven-spot, it tells me that he rested from his great work and that it was a great day. And when I look at the eight-spot, I think of the eight righteous people who were saved in the ark; there was Noah, his wife, their three sons, and their wives. And when I look at the nine-spot, I think of the ninety and nine who were safely gathered to the fold. And when I look at the ten-spot, I think of the ten great commandments that was handed down by Moses and written on tablets of stone. And when I look at the Jack, or the knave, I think of the Devil and all of his wicked ways. And when I look at the Queen, I think of the Virgin Mary, Queen of Heaven. And when I look at the King, it tells me there is but one king, the King of Kings. And now, sir, when I count the spots on my cards, I find exactly three-hundred-and-sixty-five, the exact amount of days in a year. There are twelve face cards, the exact amount of months in a year. There are four different suits, the exact amount of weeks in a month. And there are thirteen tricks, the exact amount of weeks in a quarter, plus one. So, you see, sir, my deck of cards serve me as my Bible, my prayerbook, and my calendar.''

MEDICINE PITCH

Good evening, ladies and gentlemen and welcome to the Clifton Comedy Co. We have come to your city to stay one week, bringing you clean, moral, refined entertainment which is absolutely free. We bring with us a company of fourteen performers. Each and every one an artist in his or her line. More than that, they are all ladies and gentlemen and can conduct themselves as such. There will be nothing seen, heard, said or done to mar the impunity or injure the propriety in any way, shape, form or manner, of the most fastidious little lady in the community. You may come down here every night with just as much impunity, just as much propriety as you go to church; that is if you do go to church.

Throughout the week, you're going to hear people calling me doctor. Actually, I'm not a doctor at all; I did attend Northwestern, however, for two years. But I never acquired a diploma, I'm not licensed, not allowed to make calls. Soon after, I decided I didn't want to settle down in some small town or city but I would prefer to go down into the highways and into the byways in an attempt to allay the sickness and suffering that mankind is heir to. And, friends, if you would look as I do upon that vast multitude of people that I see going to and from me daily, people that I have taken off canes, off crutches, out of the sick bed—ah, you might say, snatched off the operating table with the use of that tonic, you wouldn't blame me for preaching.

Now, we were sent here by the Finley Medicine Co. of forty-one-hundred-and-fifty-one Olive Street, St. Louis, Missouri, for the express purpose of introducing and advertising their products. And friends, we have just two products; that's the hospital tonic and the instant liniment. The hospital tonic is a harmless preparation consisting of roots, herbs, leaves, gums, berries and blossoms. Including ginseng root, dianaemma leaves, sinco salfametta berries, iron phosphate, cassian mandrake, Canadian snake root, bitter apple, Chinese dragon flower and gimico oil.

And now you're going to say, "Well, will it cure everything?" And, ladies and gentlemen, if I were to tell you we had a cure-all then I would be lying to you, and I'm not going to lie to you. Our product is good for three things and three things only. That's the stomach, the liver, and the kidneys—the three principal blood-making organs, or any disease arising therefrom, such as sour stomach, indigestion, constipation, female weaknesses, rheumatism, catarrh. Any disease arising from disorderly stomach, impure liver, deranged kidneys, with the exception of Bright's disease, of course—and if your kidney complaint has reached that stage, please don't buy a bottle, because it wouldn't do you any more good than that much rain water. And I would much, much rather you wouldn't have it.

Actually, that's all I know, as I say; those three things—the stomach, the liver, the kidneys. For example, out in back, I have a car sitting out there, a Buick, and as long as it'll run, I can drive it. But if it stops, I don't get out and try to fix it. I merely hail the first passing motorist and he may just turn over a wire, or nut or a bolt, and I'll put my foot on the starter and it will go along all right. Now, if Mr. Buick had made the car with stomach, liver, kidneys, I could have fixed it. He didn't; I don't know anything about it and I don't want to know anything about it.

Now, I've had people say to me—they'll brag about the fact they haven't taken a dose of medicine in five years, or ten years. And, friends, if they would stop and think, a person wouldn't make a remark like that, they wouldn't brag about it. Let me paint you a word picture that the very smallest boy or girl in my audience can understand. Those of us that keep house have sitting at our back door what we call a garbage can or a slop bucket. You get through with your breakfast dishes, you scrape off those dishes into that bucket. You do the same thing with your lunch, the same with your dinner. Now, when it's full you take it out, bury it, feed it to the pigs, I don't care what you do with it, but I'll ask you to do this; keep it in that capacity just for one week's time. Then I want you to see the condition that it's in. See the filth that adheres to the sides, smell the stench that comes from it and stop and think, ladies and gentlemen—I have been putting that same food into my stomach. Not for a day, a week, a month or a year but for five years or ten years, and I have never cleaned it out. And I will guarantee, friends, that the very first dose of hospital tonic will bring from your body double handfulls of filth, slime, mucus, corruption, fecal matter, maggots and even worms.

Now, not very long ago we asked the Finley Company to add one more ingredient into the product. Something that would pass a tapeworm, head and all. I am proud to say that that situation now does exist. I have several specimens back there in my office. For example, one came from a Mr. Adams, a brakeman on the Baltimore and Ohio Railroad in Sanger, Texas. He got a bottle of medicine on Monday night and on Friday he came down with that in a tin can. I washed it and measured it and it is a tapeworm that measures just over sixteen feet in length—and I have Mr. Adams' sworn statement in my trunk that he used no other medicine but the hospital tonic in the passing of that worm.

Now there is just one more thing I would like to say about the product. One thing that I think makes it stand head and shoulders above any other preparation ever offered on the market. Unfortunately, I *can't* say much before a mixed audience of ladies and gentlemen . . . But I will say this: If there is a man within a hearing of my voice who goes home tonight and he sees that poor wife, sister, mother sitting there with her head tied up and you say "What's the matter, Mary?" and she says, "Nothing, nothing's the matter, John." Don't you believe there's nothing the matter, because there is something the matter. Something she's not going to confide in you. She's not going to tell you all her troubles.

Now you know the disposition of a woman. The majority will drag themselves around as long as they can keep going and finally they break down and then you have an invalid to take care of the balance of your days. My friends, I talk to you as I would my own mother, my own folks, in my own home; and if I thought it would do any good I'd get down on this platform on my knees and I would beg you to take that woman home a bottle of tonic. Friends, if you have a woman like that at home tonight and you see she's on the toboggan, on the downhill path, and you want to bring the roses back to her cheeks, make her step pick up, make her feel like she should again, you will take my advice and take her home a bottle of that tonic. Oh friends, if there is one drop of blood in your body that beats warm for that poor dear woman, take my advice . . . Take her home a bottle of that tonic!

Now, the price—the price is smallest part of it. It's a dollar a bottle and with every bottle we will include 100 votes for the most popular lady or baby in the community. I'm going to have the agents pass among you just once—those of you who are seated just raise your hand. And those of you sitting back in the cars if you'll turn on your lights, we'll be glad to wait on you. It's a dollar a bottle, and 100 votes with each bottle. I thank you ladies and gentlemen. I thank you.

CANDY SALE PITCH

Good evening, ladies and gentlemen. Tonight we're introducing the new prize candy confection entitled "Candy Dates." Now each and every package does indeed contain a prize put out by the Gordon Howard Candy Company of Kansas City, Missouri. However, many of these prizes are much too large to be contained within the packages and have coupons calling for them up on the stage. Now, these coupons call for various articles such as safety razors, silk hose, silk lingerie, opera glasses, field glasses, pen and pencil sets, garter and hose sets, boxes of stationery, tilt-top tables and many other valuable and useful articles, and we're putting them out at the advertising price of just 25¢ each. I'm going to have the agents pass among you just once and those of you that are seated raise your hands and those of you in the cars if you'll turn on your lights we'll be glad to wait on you. It's 25¢, raise your hands, turn on your lights and we'll be glad to wait on you. Open your packages, bring up your coupons.

THE GEEK PITCH

Ladies and gentlemen, you are now standing in front of the feature attraction of the entire midway, the home of that strangest of all strange creatures, that girl whom we call Neola. Now, Neola was brought here during the great evolution trials that took place in Dayton, Tennessee, in 1925 between the late William Jennings Bryan and Clarence Darrow, that great criminal lawyer. She was examined by some of our leading psychiatrists; Dr. Mullen at the Dept. of Psychiatry, Columbia, studied upon her and he claimed her to have less intelligence, less brains than that of the chimpanzee or monkey family.

Now she was first found by a Dr. Carter, that great antiquarian, explorer, and trapper, who was exploring in the center of deep dark caves in the lowlands or swamp regions of Abyssinia. He heard this strange tale from some fanatical natives, who claimed to have seen an animal in the center of that cave. Investigating their story he found it to be fact; yet he found, not an animal, but a human being, crouched upon a huge flat rock, exactly as you're going to see her in there tonight, completely surrounded by hissing, seething monsters, some larger than a man's upper arm. Some that could crush a human being with just one coil of those enormous bodies, as easily as you or I could crush a piece of food between our teeth!

From a point of vantage he watched her; she would first tease, tanatalize and torment them until they would strike in their wildest of fury, biting her all over her miserable body, upon the arms, the limbs, the cheeks, even upon the tongue, until the blood would actually course from those wounds just as you would pour water from a glass. Then often, to avenge herself, she would pick up one of the larger reptiles, place the head between those massive jaws, bite off the head, peel down the skin and proceed to devour it, head, hide, tail and all, as you or I would peel a banana.

Now, ladies and gentlemen, let me paint you a word picture of that strange girl. She stands three feet tall; she has long, long arms that hang way down below the knees; eyes that actually pop out and glare just like two red hot coals of fire. But, I think—and I think you'll agree with me when you see her—that the most peculiar thing about her is the shape of the head. The head tapers at the top just like that of a coconut. She doesn't speak any language, doesn't know any creed, neither walks nor talks, just creeps, crawls and spends her lifetime down in that steel-bound cage, down in that steel arena, where you wouldn't expect a dog to live for an hour.

Now all afternoon you've been asking when and what time are you going to feed her; and, ladies and gentlemen, I am happy to say that that time has now arrived. Once on exhibition—in fact, on this very performance—I am going to feed her just as you'd see her in her own native land, Abyssinia, in the North of Africa. And when I throw that live chicken down deep into that steel-bound cage, that same chicken you see me there now holding, you're going to see a most amazing change come over the old woman. The eyes will dilate, the pupils glow just like two red hot coals of fire. You're going to hear her emit just one long, soul-searing scream and leap clear across that steel-bound arena. She'll catch that bird with the two massive jaws—and speaking of jaws, ladies and gentlemen, she has a single row of teeth on the upper jaw, and a double row on the lower jaw. She'll bite off the head with the long and tusky teeth and then—and then, ladies and gentlemen, as repulsive as it may sound, she will proceed to suck, drain and draw every drop of blood from that bleeding, throbbing, quivering, pulsating body with the very same relish that you or I would suck the juice of an orange. One of the most disgusting, one of the most repulsive, one of the most revolting and, yet I'll say, one of the most interesting sights you've ever seen in all of your life.

Now, it's natural to doubt the word of a showman. But let me say this, if you go in there tonight and you fail to find her exactly as I represented her in every way, in every shape, form or manner, then I'll beg you, I'll plead with you, in fact, I'll implore you to come back to the pay box and I'll refund your money as cheerfully as I've taken it from you. As you all know, the admission is 25¢ for the adults and 10¢ for the little ones. Tonight I'm going to turn back the pages of time, I'm going to make children out of all of you. I'll say this: for a period of three minutes and three minutes only, if you can lay as much as a dime, that's just 10¢ upon that pay box, everybody goes—ladies, gentlemen, children—all go on a 10¢ ticket. It's now way past feeding time and I am going to feed her within three minutes, whether one of you go, all of you go, or none of you go. Thank you ladies and gentlemen. You can get tickets here, get tickets here. (*Calling inside.*) Hold it, doctor, don't feed her just yet.

JOSH BILLINGS' LECTURE

Ladies and Gentlemen:

I hope you are all well. (*Looking over his glasses.*)

Thare is lots ov folks who eat well and drink well, and yet are sick all the time. Theze are the folks who alwuz "enjoy poor health."

Then I kno lots ov people whoze only reckomendashun iz, that they are healthy—so iz an onion. (*Laughter.*)

The subject of my lecture is Milk—plain M-i-l-k.

The best thing I've ever seen on milk is cream. (*Laughter.*)

That's right. (*Joining.*) "People of good sense" are thoze whoze opinyuns agree with ours. (*Laughter.*)

People who agree with you never bore you. The shortest way to a woman's harte iz to praze her baby and her bonnet, and to a man's harte to praze hiz watch, hiz horse and hiz lectur.

Elizar Perkins sez a man iz a bore when he talks so much about hisself that you kant talk about yourself. (*Laughter.*)

Still I shall go on talking.

Comik lekturing iz an unkommon pesky thing to do.

It iz more unsarting than the rat ketching bizzness az a means ov grace, or az a means ov livelyhood.

Most enny boddy thinks they kan do it, and this iz jist what makes it so bothersum tew do.

When it iz did jist enuff, it iz a terifik success, but when it iz overdid, it iz like a burnt slapjax, very impertinent.

Thare aint but phew good judges ov humor, and they all differ about it.

If a lekturer trys tew be phunny, he iz like a hoss trying to trot backwards, pretty apt tew trod on himself. (*Laughter.*)

Humor must fall out ov a man's mouth, like musik out ov a bobalink, or like a yung bird ov its nest, when it iz feathered enuff to fly.

Whenever a man haz made up hiz mind that he iz a wit, then he iz mistaken without remedy, but whenever the publick haz made up their mind that he haz got the disease, then he haz got it sure.

Individuals never git this thing right, the publick never git it wrong.

Humor iz wit with a rooster's tail feathers stuck in its cap, and wit iz wisdom in tight harness.

If a man is a genuine humorist, he iz superior to the bulk ov hiz audience, and will often hev tew take hiz pay for hiz services in thinking so.

Altho fun iz designed for the millyun, and ethiks for the few, it iz az true az molasses, that most all aujiences hav their bell wethers, people who show the others the crack whare the joke cums laffing in. (Where are they to-night?) (*Laughter.*)

I hav known popular aujences deprived ov all plezzure during the recital ov a comik lektur, just bekauze the right man, or the right woman, want thare tew point out the mellow places.

The man who iz anxious tew git before an aujience, with what he calls a comik lektur, ought tew be put immediately in the stocks, so that he kant do it, for he iz a dangerous person tew git loose, and will do sum damage.

It iz a very pleazant bizzness tew make people laff, but thare iz much odds whether they laff at you, or laff at what you say.

When a man laffs at yu, he duz it because it makes him feel superior to you, but when yu pleaze him with what yu have uttered, he admits that yu are superior tew him. (*Applause.*)

The only reazon whi a monkey alwus kreates a sensashun whareever he goes, is simply bekauze—he is a monkey.

Everyboddy feels az tho they had a right tew criticize a comik lectur, and most ov them do it jist az a mule criticizes things, by shutting up both eyes and letting drive with hiz two behind leggs. (*Laughter.*)

One ov the meanest things in the comik lektring employment that a man haz to do, iz tew try and make that large class ov hiz aujience laff whom the Lord never intended should laff.

Thare is sum who laff az eazy and az natral az the birds do, but most ov mankind laff like a hand organ—if yu expect tew git a lively tune out ov it yu hav got tew grind for it.

In delivering a comik lektur it iz a good general rule to stop sudden, sometime before yu git through.

This brings me to Long branch.

Long branch iz a work ov natur, and iz a good job. It iz a summer spot for men, wimmin and children, espeshily the latter. Children are az plenty here, and az sweet az flowers, in an out door gardin. I put up at the Oshun Hotel the last time i was thare, and I put up more than I ought to. Mi wife puts up a good deal with me at the same hotel, it iz an old-fashioned way we have ov doing things. She allways goes with me, to fashionable resorts, whare young widows are enny ways plenty, to put me on mi guard, for I'm one ov the easyest creatures on reckord to be impozed upon, espeshily bi yung widders. She is an ornament to her sex, mi wife iz. I would like to see a young widder, or even an old one, git the start cv me, when mi wife iz around. (*Laughter.*) If I just step out sudden, to get a weak lemonade, to cool mi akeing brow, mi wife goes to the end ov the verandy with me, and waits for me, and if i go down on-to the beach to astronomize just a little, all alone, bi moonlite, she stands on the bluff, like a beakon lite, to warn me ov the breakers.

The biggest thing they hav got at Long branch, for the present, iz the pool ov water, in front ov the hotels. This pool iz sed bi good judges to be 3,000 miles in length, and in sum places 5 miles thick. Into this pool, every day at ten o'klock, the folks all retire, males, females, and widders, promiskuss. The scenery here iz grand, especially the pool, and the air iz az bracing az a milk puntch. Drinks are reasonable here, espeshily out ov the pool, and the last touch ov civilizashun haz reached here also, sum enterprising mishionary haz just opened a klub house, whare all kind ov gamvling iz taught.

Long branch iz a healthy place.

Men and women here, if they ain't too lazy, liv sumtimes till they are eighty, and destroy the time a good deal as follows: The fust thirty years they spend throwing stuns at a mark, the seckond thirty they spend in examining the mark tew see whare the stuns hit, and the remainder is divided in cussing the stun-throwing bizziness, and nussing the rumatizz.

A man never gits to be a fust klass phool until he haz reached seventy years, and falls in luv with a bar maid of 19, and marrys her, and then,— * * * * *Here he took out his Waterbury watch, and remarked, as he wound it up, "You kant do two things to wonst." (*Great laughter.*)

I luv a Rooster for two things. One iz the crow that iz in him, and the other iz, the spurs that are on him, to bak up the crow with.

There was a little disturbance in the gallery now, and Uncle Josh looked over his glasses and remarked:

"Yung man, please set down, and keep still, yu will hav plenty ov chances yet to make a phool ov yurself before yu die." (*Laughter.*)

The man or mule who can't do any hurt in this world kan't do any good. (*Laughter.*)

This brings me to the Mule—the pashunt mule. The mule is pashunt because he is ashamed of hisself. (*Laughter.*) The mule is a haf hoss and haf jackass, and then kums tu a full stop, natur diskovering her mistake. Tha weigh more accordin tu their heft than enny other creeter, except a crowbar. Tha kant heer enny quicker nor further than the hoss, yet their ears are big enuff fur snowshoes. You kan trust them with enny one whose life aint worth more than the mule's. The only way tu keep them into a paster is tu turn them into a medder jineing and let them jump out. (*Laughter.*) Tha are reddy for use jest as soon as tha will do tu abuse. Tha aint got enny friends, and will live on huckleberry bush, with an akasional chance at Kanada thissels. Tha are a modern invention. Tha sell fur more money than enny other domestic animal. You kant tell their age by looking into their mouth enny more than you could a Mexican cannon. Tha never have no disease that a good club won't heal. If tha ever die tha must come right to life agin, fur I never herd nobody say "ded mule." I never owned one, nor never mean to, unless there is a United States law passed requiring it. I have seen educated mules in a sircuss. Tha could kick and bite tremenjis . . . Enny man who is willing to drive a mule ought to be exempt by law from running for the legislatur. Tha are the strongest creeters on arth, and heaviest according tu their size. I herd of one who fell oph from the tow-path of the Eri canawl, and sunk as soon as he touched bottom, but he kept on towing the boat tu the next stashun, breathing through his ears, which was out of the water about two feet six inches. I didn't see this did, but Bill Harding told me of it, and I never knew Bill Harding tu lie unless he could make something out of it. There is but one other animal that kan do more kicking than a mule, and that is a Quire Singer. (*Laughter.*) A quire singer giggles during the sermon and kicks the rest of the week. My advice to quire singers is as follows:

Put your hair in cirl papers every Friday nite soze to have it in good shape Sunday morning. If your daddy is rich you can but some store hair. If he is very rich buy some more and build it up high onto your head; then get a high-priced bunnit that runs up very high at the high part of it, and get the milliner to plant some high-grown artificials onto the highest part of it. This will help you sing high, as soprano is the highest part.

When the tune is giv out, don't pay attention to it, and then giggle. Giggle a good eel.

Whisper to the girl next to you that Em Jones, which sets on the 2nd seet from the front on the left-hand side, has her bunnit with the same color exact she had last year, and then put your book to your face and giggle.

Object to every tune unless there is a solow into it for the soprano. Coff and hem a good eel before you begin to sing.

When you sing a solow shake the artificials off your bunnit, and when you come to a high tone brace yourself back a little, twist your head to one side and open your mouth the widest on that side, shet the eyes on the same side jest a triphle, and then put in for dear life.

When the preacher gets under hed way with his preachin, write a note on the blank leaf into the fourth part of your note book. That's what the blank leaf was made for. Git sumbody to pass the note to sumbody else, and you watch them while they read it, and then giggle. (*Laughter.*)

If anybody talks or laffs in the congregashun, and the preacher takes notis of it, that's a good chants for you to giggle, and you ought to giggle a great eel. The preacher darsent say any thing to you bekaus you are in the quire, and he can't run the meetin' house at both ends without the quire. If you had a bow before you went into the quire, give him the mitten—you ought to have somebody better now.

Don't forget to giggle.

The quire singer suggests the bumble-bee.

The bumble-bee iz more artistic than the mule and as busy as a quire singer. The bumble-bee iz a kind ov big fly who goes muttering and swearing around the lots during the summer looking after little boys to sting them, and stealing hunny out ov the dandylions and thissels. Like the mule, he iz mad all the time about sumthing, and don't seem to kare a kuss what people think ov him.

A skool boy will studdy harder enny time to find bumble-bee's nest than he will to get hiz lesson in arithmetik, and when he haz found it, and got the hunny out ov it, and got badly stung into the bargin, he finds thare aint mutch margin in it. Next to poor molassis, bumble-bee hunny iz the poorest kind ov sweetmeats in market. Bumble-bees have allwuss been in fashion, and probably allwuss will be, but whare the fun or proffit lays in them, i never could cypher out. The proffit don't seem to be in the hunny, nor in the bumble-bee neither. They bild their nest in the ground, or enny whare else they take a noshun too, and ain't afrade to fite a whole distrikt skool, if they meddle with them. I don't blame the bumble-bee, nor enny other fellow, for defending hiz sugar: it iz the fust, and last law of natur, and i hope the law won't never run out. The smartest thing about the bumble-bee iz their stinger. (*Laughter.*)

Speaking of smart things brings me to the hornet:

The hornet is an inflamibel buzzer, sudden in hiz impreshuns and hasty in his conclusion, or end.

Hiz natral disposishen iz a warm cross between red pepper in the pod and fusil oil, and hiz moral bias iz, "git out ov mi way."

They have a long, black boddy, divided in the middle by a waist spot, but their phisikal importance lays at the terminus of their subburb, in the shape ov a javelin.

This javelin iz alwuz loaded, and stands reddy to unload at a minuit's warning, and enters a man az still az thought, az spry az litening, and az full ov melankolly az the toothake.

Hornets never argy a case; they settle awl ov their differences ov opinyon by letting their javelin fly, and are az certain to hit az a mule iz.

This testy kritter lives in congregations numbering about 100 souls, but whether they are mail or female, or conservative, or matched in bonds ov wedlock, or whether they are Mormons, and a good many ov them kling together and keep one husband to save expense, I don't kno nor don't kare. I never have examined their habits much, I never konsidered it healthy.

Hornets build their nests wherever they take a noshun to, and seldom are disturbed, for what would it profit man tew kill 99 hornets and hav the 100th one hit him with hiz javelin? (*Laughter.*)

They bild their nests ov papre, without enny windows to them or back doors. They have but one place ov admission, and the nest iz the shape ov an overgrown pineapple, and is cut up into just as many bedrooms as there iz hornets.

It iz very simple to make a hornet's nest if yu kan (*laughter*) but it will wager enny man 300 dollars he kant bild one that he could sell to a hornet for half price.

Hornets are as bizzy as their second couzins, the bee, but what they are about the Lord only knows; they don't lay up enny honey, nor enny money; they seem to be bizzy only jist for the sake ov working all the time; they are alwus in as mutch ov a hurry as tho they waz going for a dokter.

I suppose this uneasy world would grind around on its axle-tree onst in 24 hours, even ef thare went enny hornets, but hornets must be good for sumthing, but I kant think now what it iz.

Thare haint been a bug made yet in vain, nor one that want a good job; there is ever lots of human men loafing around the blacksmith shops, and cider mills, all over the country, that don't seem to be necessary for anything but to beg plug tobacco and swear, and steal water melons, but yu let the cholera break at once, and then yu will see the wisdom of having jist sich men laying around; they help count. (*Laughter.*)

Next tew the cockroach, who stands tew the head, the hornet haz got the most waste stummuk, in reference tew the rest of hiz boddy, than any of the insek populashun, and here iz another mystery; what on'arth duz a hornet want so much reserved corps for?

I have jist thought-tew carry his javelin in; thus yu see, the more we diskover about things the more we are apt to know.

It iz always a good purchase tew pay out our last surviving dollar for wisdum, and wisdum iz like the misterious hen's egg; it ain't laid in yure hand, but iz laid away under the barn, and yu have got to sarch for it.

The hornet iz an unsoshall kuss, he iz more haughty than he is proud, he is a thourough-bred bug, but his breeding and refinement has made him like sum other folks I know ov, dissatisfied with himself and every boddy else, too much good breeding ackts this way sometimes.

Hornets are long-lived- I kant state jist how long their lives are, but I know from instink and observashen that enny krittur, be he bug or be he devil, who iz mad all the time, and stings every good chance he kan git, generally outlives all his nabers.

The only good way tew git at the exact fiteing weight of the hornet is tew tutch him, let him hit you once with his javelin, and you will be willing to testify in court that somebody run a one-tined pitchfork into yer; and as for grit, i will state for the informashun of thoze who haven't had a chance tew lay in their vermin wisdum az freely az I hav, that one single hornet, who feels well, will brake up a large camp-meeting. (*Laughter.*)

What the hornets do for amuzement is another question i kant answer, but sum ov the best read and heavyest thinkers among the naturalists say they have target excursions, and heave their javelins at a mark; but I don't imbide this assershun raw, for i never knu enny body so bitter at heart as the hornets are, to waste a blow.

Thare iz one thing that a hornet duz that i will give him credit for on my books—he alwuz attends tew his own bizziness, and won't allow any boddy else tew attend tew it, and what he duz iz alwuz a good job; you never see them altering enny thing; if they make enny mistakes, it is after dark, and aint seen.

If the hornets made half az menny blunders az the men do, even with their javelins, every boddy wouldlaff at them.

Hornets are clear in another way, they hav found out, by trieing it, that all they can git in this world, and brag on, is their vittles and clothes, and yu never see one standing on the corner ov a street, with a twenty-six inch face on, bekause sum bank had run oph and took their money with him.

In ending oph this essa, i will cum tew a stop by concluding, that if hornets was a little more pensive, and not so darned peremptory with their javelins, they might be guilty of less wisdum, but more charity.

This brings me to Flirts.

Flirts are like hornets, only men like to be stung by them.

Some old bachelors git after a flirt, and don't travel as fast as she doz, and then concludes awl the female group are hard to ketch, and good for nothing when they are ketched.

A flirt is a rough thing to overhaul unless the right dog gets after her, and then they make the very best of wives.

When a flirt really is in love, she is as powerless as a mown daisy. (*Laughter.*)

Her impudence then changes into modesty, her cunning into fears, her spurs into a halter, and her pruning-hook into a cradle.

The best way to ketch a flirt is tew travel the other way from which they are going, or sit down on the ground and whistle some lively tune till the flirt comes round. (*Laughter.*)

Old bachelors make the flirts and then the flirts get more than even, by making the old bachelors.

A majority of flirts get married finally, for they hev a great quantity of the most dainty tidbits of woman's nature, and alwus have shrewness to back up their sweetness.

Flirts don't deal in po'try and water grewel; they have got to hev brains, or else somebody would trade them out of their capital at the first sweep.

Disappointed luv must uv course be oll on one side; this ain't any more excuse fur being an old bachelor than it iz fur a man to quit all kinds of manual labor, jist out uv spite, and jine a poor-house bekase he kant lift a tun at one pop.

An old bachelor will brag about his freedom to you, his relief from anxiety, hiz indipendence. This iz a dead beat, past resurrection, for everybody knows there ain't a more anxious dupe than he iz. All his dreams are charcoal sketches of boarding-school misses; he dresses, greases hiz hair, paints his grizzly mustache, cultivates bunyons and corns, to please his captains, the wimmen, and only gets laffed at fur hiz pains.

I tried being an old bachelor till I wuz about twenty years old, and came very near dieing a dozen times. I had more sharp pain in one year than I hev had since, put it all in a heap. I was in a lively fever all the time.

I have preached to you about flirts (phemale), and now I will tell you about Dandies.

The first dandy was made by Dame Nature, out of the refuse matter left from making Adam and Eve. He was concocted with a bouquet in one hand and a looking-glass in the other. His heart was dissected in the thirteenth-century, and found to be a pincushion full of butterflies and sawdust. He never falls in love, for to love requires both brains and a soul, and the dandy has neither. He is a long-lived bird; he has no courage, never marries, has no virtues, and is never guilty of first-class vices.

What about Marriage?

They say love iz blind, but a good many fellows see more in their sweethearts than I can.

Marriage is a fair transaction on the face ov it.

But thare iz quite too often put-up jobs in it.

It is an old institushun—older than the pyramids, and az phull ov hyrogliphics that nobody can parse.

History holds its tongue who the pair waz who fust put on silken harness, and promised to work kind in it, thru thick and thin, up hill and down, and on the level, rain or shine, survive or perish, sink or swim, drown or flote.

But whoever they waz, they must hev made a good thing out of it, or so menny ov their posterity would not hev harnessed up since and drove out.

Thare iz a grate moral grip to marriage; it iz the mortar that holds the sooshul bricks together.

But thare ain't but darn few pholks who put their money in matrimony who could set down and give a good written opinyun whi on airth they come to did it.

This iz a grate proof that it iz one ov them natral kind ov acksidents that must happen, jist az birdz fly out ov the nest, when they hev featherz enuff, without being able tew tell why.

Sum marry for buty, and never diskover their mistake: this is lucky.

Sum marry for money, and don't see it.

Sum marry for pedigree, and feel big for six months; and then very sensibly cum tew the conclusion that pedigree ain't no better than skim-milk.

Sum marry bekawze they have been highsted sum where else; this iz a cross match, a bay and a sorrel; pride may make it endurable.

Sum marry for luv, without a cent in their pockets, nor a friend in the world, nor a drop ov pedigree. This looks desperate, but it iz the strength of the game.

If marrying for luv ain't a success, then matrimony is a ded beet.

Sum marry because they think wimmen will be scarce next year, and live tew wonder how the crop holdz out.

Sum marry tew get rid ov themselves, and discover that the game waz one that two could play at, and neither win.

Sum marry the second time tew get even, and find it a gambling game —the more they put down the less they take up.

Sum marry, tew be happy, and, not finding it, wonder where all the happiness goes to when it dies.

Sum marry, they can't tell why, and live they can't tell how.

Almost every boddy gets married, and it is a good joke.

Sum marry in haste, and then sit down and think it carefully over.

Sum think it over careful fust, and then set down and marry.

Both ways are right, if they hit the mark.

Sum marry rakes tew convert them. This iz a little risky, and takes a smart missionary to do it.

Sum marry coquetts. This iz like buying a poor farm heavily mortgaged, and working the balance of your days to clear oph the mortgages.

Married life haz its chances, and this iz just what gives it its flavor. Every boddy luvs tew phool with the chances, bekawze every boddy expects tew win. But I am authorized tew state that every boddy don't win.

But, after all, married life iz full az certain az the dry goods bizness.

Kno man kan tell jist what calico haz made up its mind tew do next.

Calico don't kno even herself.

Dry goods ov all kinds iz the child ov circumstansis.

Sum never marry, but this iz jist ez risky; the diseaze iz the same, with another name to.

The man who stands on the banks shivering, and dassent, iz more apt tew ketch cold than him who pitches hiz head fust into the river.

Thare iz but few who never marry bekawze they won't—they all hankar, and most ov them starve with bread before them (spread on both sides), jist for the lack ov grit.

Marry young! iz mi motto.

I hev tried it, and I know what I am talking about.

If enny boddy asks you whi you got married (if it needs be), tell him "yu don't recollekt."

Marriage iz a safe way to gamble—if yu win, yu win a pile, and if yu loze, yu don't loze enny thing, only the privilege of living dismally alone and soaking your own feet.

I repeat it, in italics, *marry young!*

There iz but one good excuse for a marriage late in life, and that is—a second marriage.

When you are married, don't swap with your mother-in-law, unless yu kin afford to give her the big end of the trade. Say "how are you" to every boddy. Kultivate modesty, but mind and keep a good stock of impudence on hand. Be charitable—three-cent pieces were made on purpose. It costs more to borry than it does to buy. Ef a man flatters yu, yu can kalkerlate he is a roge, or yu are a fule. Be more anxus about the pedigree yur going to leave than yu are about the wun somebody's going to leave you. Sin is like weeds—self-sone and sure to cum. Two lovers, like two armies, generally get along quietly until they are engaged.

I will now give young men my advice about getting married.

Find a girl that iz 19 years old last May, about the right hight with a blue eye, and dark-brown hair and white teeth.

Let the girl be good to look at, not too phond of musik, a firm disbeleaver in ghosts, and one ov six children in the same family.

Look well tew the karakter ov her father; see that he is not the member ov enny klub, don't bet on elekshuns, and gits shaved at least 3 times a week.

Find out all about her mother, see if she haz got a heap ov good common sense, studdy well her likes and dislikes, eat sum ov her hum-made bread and apple dumplins, notiss whether she abuzes all ov her nabors, and don't fail tew observe whether her dresses are last year's ones fixt over.

If you are satisfied that the mother would make the right kind ov a mother-in-law, yu kan safely konklude that the dauter would make the right kind of a wife. (*Applause.*)

What about courtin'?

Courting is a luxury, it is sallad, it is ise water, it is a beveridge, it is the pla spell ov the soul.

The man who has never courted haz lived in vain; he haz bin a blind man amung landskapes and watershapes; he haz bin a deff man in the land ov hand orgins, and by the side ov murmuring canals. (*Laughter.*)

Courting iz like 2 little springs ov soft water that steal out from under a rock at the fut ov a mountain and run down the hill side by side singing and dansing and spatering each uther, eddying and frothing and kaskading, now hiding under bank, now full ov sun and now full of shadder, till bime by tha jine and then tha go slow. (*Laughter.*)

I am in favor of long courting; it gives the parties a chance to find out each uther's trump kards; it iz good exercise, and is jist as innersent as 2 merino lambs.

Courting iz like strawberries and cream, wants tew be did slow, then yu git the flavor.

Az a ginral thing i wouldn't brag on uther gals mutch when i waz courting, it mite look az tho yu knu tew mutch.

If yu will court 3 years in this wa, awl the time on the square, if yu don't sa it iz a leettle the slikest time in yure life, yu kan git measured for a hat at my expense, and pa for it.

Don't court for munny, nor buty, nor relashuns, theze things are jist about az onsartin as the kerosene ile refining bissness, libel tew git out ov repair and bust at enny minnit.

Court a gal for fun, for the luv yu bear her, for the vartue and bissness thare is in her; court her for a wife and for a mother; court her as yu wud court a farm— for the strength ov the sile and the parfeckshun ov the title; court her as tho' she want a fule, and yu a nuther; court her in the kitchen, in the parlor, over the wash tub, and at the pianner; court this wa, yung man, and if yu don't git a good wife and she don't git a good hustband, the falt won't be in the courting.

Yung man, yu kan rely upon Josh Billings, and if yu kant make these rules wurk, jist send for him, and he will sho yu how the thing is did, and it shant kost you a cent.

I will now give the following Advice to Lecture Committees outside of this town:

1. Don't hire enny man tew lectur for yu (never mind how moral he iz) unless yu kan make munny on him.

2. Selekt 10 ov yure best lookin and most talking members tew meet the lekturer at the depot.

3. Don't fail tew tell the lekturer at least 14 times on yure way from the depot tew the hotel that yu hav got the smartest town in kreashun, and sevral men in it that are wuth over a millyun.

4. When yu reach the hotel introduce the lekturer immejiately to at least 25 ov yure fust-klass citizens, if you hav tew send out for them.

5. When the lekturer's room iz reddy go with him in masse to hiz room and remind him 4 or 5 times that yu had over 3 thousand people in yure city at the last censuss, and are a talking about having an opera house.

6. Don't leave the lekturer alone in his room over 15 minits at once; he might take a drink out ov his flask on the sli if yu did.

7. When yu introjuce the lekturer tew the aujience don't fail tew make a speech ten or twelve feet long, occupying a haff an hour, and if yu kan ring in sumthing about the growth ov yure butiful sitty, so mutch the better. (*Laughter.*)

8. Always seat 9 or 10 ov the kommitty on the stage, and then if it iz a kommik lektur, and the kommitty don't laff a good deal, the aujience will konklude that the lektur iz a failure; and if they do laff a good deal, the aujience will konklude they are stool-pigeons. (*Laughter.*)

9. Jist az soon az the lectur is thru bring 75 or 80 ov the richest ov yure populashun up onto the stage and let them squeeze the hand and exchange talk with the lekturer.

10. Go with the lekturer from the hall tew hiz room in a bunch, and remind him once or twice more on the way that yure sitty iz a growing very rapidly, and ask him if he don't think so.

11. If the lekturer should inquire how the comik lekturers had succeeded who had preceded him, don't forget tew tell him that they were all failures. This will enable him tew guess what they will say about him just az soon az he gits out ov town. (*Laughter.*)

12. If the lekturer's fee should be a hundred dollars or more, don't hesitate, in old, lop-eared one-dollar bills, with a liberal sandwitching ov tobbakko-stained shinplasters.

13. I forgot tew say that fust thing yu should tell a lekturer, after yu had sufficiently informed him ov the immense growth ov yure citty, iz that yure people are not edukated up tew lekturs yet, but are grate on nigger-minstrels.

14. Never fail tew ask the lekturer whare he finds the most appreshiated aujiences, and he won't fail tew tell yu (if he iz an honest man) that thare ain't no state in the Union that begins tew kompare with yures.

15. Let 15 or 20 ov yure kommitty go with the lekturer, next morning, tew the kars, and az each one shakes hands with him with a kind ov deth grip, don't forget tew state that yure citty iz growing very mutch in people.

16. If the night iz wet, and the inkum ov the house won't pay expenses, don't hesitate tew make it pay by taking a chunk out ov the lekturer's fee. The lekturers all like this, but they are too modest, as a klass, tew say so.

17. I know ov several other good rules tew follow, but the abuv will do

tew begin with.

Your Schoolmaster will tell you the rest.

Thare iz one man in this world to whom i alwus take oph mi hat, and remain uncovered untill he gits safely by, and that iz the distrikt skoolmaster.

When I meet him, I look upon him az a martyr just returning from the stake, or on hiz way thare tew be cooked.

He leads a more lonesum and single life than an old bachelor, and a more anxious one than an old maid.

He iz remembered jist about az long and affektionately az a gide board iz by a traveling pack pedlar.

If he undertakes tew make his skollars luv him, the chances are he will neglekt their larning; and if he don't lick them now and then pretty often, they will soon lick him. (*Laughter.*)

The distrikt skoolmaster hain't got a friend on the flat side ov earth. The boys snow-ball him during recess; the girls put water in hiz hair die; and the skool committee make him work for haff the money a bartender gits, and board him around the naberhood, whare they giv him rhy coffee, sweetened with mollassis, tew drink, and kodfish bawls 3 times a day for vittles. (*Laughter.*)

And, with all this abuse, I never heard ov a distrikt skoolmaster swareing enny thing louder than—Condem it.

Don't talk tew me about the pashunce ov anshunt Job.

Job had pretty plenty ov biles all over him, no doubt, but they were all ov one breed.

Every yung one in a distrikt skool iz a bile ov a diffrent breed, and each one needs a diffrent kind ov poultiss tew git a good head on them.

A distrikt skoolmaster, who duz a square job and takes hiz codfish bawls reverently, iz a better man today tew hav lieing around loose than Solomon would be arrayed in all ov his glory.

Solomon waz better at writing proverbs and manageing a large family, than he would be tew navigate a distrikt skool hous.

Enny man who haz kept a distrikt skool for ten years, and boarded aroung the naberhood, ought tew be made a mager gineral, and hav a penshun for the rest ov his natral days, and a hoss and waggin tew do hiz going around in.

But, az a genral consequence, a distrikt skoolmaster hain't got any more warm friends than an old blind fox houn haz.

He iz jist az welkum az a tax gatherer iz.

He iz respekted a good deal az a man iz whom we owe a debt ov 50 dollars to and don't mean tew pay.

He goes through life on a back road, az poor az a wood sled, and finally iz missed—but what ever bekums ov hiz remains, i kant tell.

Fortunately he iz not often a sensitive man; if he waz, he couldn't enny more keep a distrikt skool than he could file a kross kut saw. (*Laughter.*)

Whi iz it that theze men and wimmen, who pashuntly and with crazed brain teach our remorseless brats the tejus meaning ov the alphabet, who take the fust welding heat on their destinys, who lay the stepping stones and enkuttage them tew mount upwards, who hav dun more hard and mean work than enny klass on the futstool, who have prayed over the reprobate, strengthened the timid, restrained the outrageous, and flattered the imbecile, who hav lived on kodfish and vile coffee, and hain't been heard to sware—whi iz it that they are treated like a vagrant fiddler, danced to for a night, paid oph in the morning, and eagerly forgotten.

I had rather burn a coal pit, or keep the flys out ov a butcher's shop in the month of August, than meddle with the distrikt skool bizzness. (*Applause.*)

I propose now to close by making Twelve Square Remarks, to-wit:

1. A broken reputashun iz like a broken vase; it may be mended, but allways shows where the krak was.

2. If you kant trust a man for the full amount, let him skip. This trying to git an average on honesty haz allways bin a failure.

3. Thare iz no treachery in silence; silence is a hard argument to beat.

4. Don't mistake habits for karacter. The men ov the most karacter hav the fewest habits.

5. Thare iz cheats in all things; even pizen is adulterated.

6. The man who iz thoroughly polite iz 2-thirds ov a Christian, enny how.

7. Kindness iz an instinkt, politeness only an art.

8. Thare iz a great deal ov learning in this world, which iz nothing more than trying to prove what we don't understand.

9. Mi dear boy, thare are but few who kan kommence at the middle ov the ladder and reach the top; and probably you and I don't belong to that number.

10. One ov the biggest mistakes made yet iz made by the man who thinks he iz temperate, just becauze he puts more water in his whiskey than his nabor does.

11. The best medicine I know ov for the rumatism jz to thank the Lord —that it aint the gout. (*Laughter.*)

12. Remember the poor. It costs nothing. (*Laughter.*)

THE DIALOGUE AND THE BIT

In the bit, a joke was expanded into a small routine for two of three performers. Often, the expansion amounted to little more than the creation of a slender comic bracketing device which served to frame the work of a pair of performers, sometimes aided by a supernumerary or two. Usually the principal performers played some variation on the classic concept of Comic and Straight Man (or Feeder as he was sometimes called), with the Straight setting up the various gags for his partner. Take, for example, a brief "Interruption" scene with a "legal" theme. The Straight is just beginning to sing a song when the Comic appears from the wings carrying a case of beer bottles. "What are you doing?" asks the Straight. "Taking my case to court," responds the Comic as he exits. The Straight thinks it over and once again begins to sing. Again the Comic enters, this time carrying both the beer and a step ladder. The frustrated singer stops. "What are you doing now?" he inquires. "Taking my case to a higher court," the Comic says as he disappears into the wings a second time. Yet again the Straight starts his song, and again the Comic appears, now clutching an empty coat hanger. "What is it this time?" asks the enraged Straight. "I lost my suit," the Comic says. Blackout.

A somewhat more elaborate and integrated bit is suggested by a scenario in the Chuck Callahan collection of vaudeville and burlesque material, an assemblage of some 300 manuscript bits and sketches at the Hampden-Booth Library in New York City. The bit involves Cohn, a Jewish-dialect Comic; a Straight; and an Irish Second Comedian. Called "Brown the Butcher" it is related to the famous "Flugel Street" bit performed by Abbott and Costello, as well as to a medicine show bit called "Down on the Hats" which was used for many years by Mae Noell's family company.

The Callahan version reads: "In this bit Cohn wears Derby hat. Str. and Irish enter. Take two chairs down to first ent. Str. starts to tell story about Brown the Butcher having a fight with his chauffeur on his way to a party. Brown was all dressed up in a full dressed suit and a silk hat. (Com. takes off hat and places it between them on floor.) Str. says Brown arrived at a party in a big car and the driver got out and opened the door and when Brown stepped out of the car he stepped in a puddle of water. Slipped and fell, spoiling the dress suit. This made Brown sore and he hit the driver, and the driver grabbed Brown's hat and threw it on the ground and started to jump up and down on it. (Bus. of jumping on Com. Hat. Com. laughs all the time and doesn't notice hat. Straight sits down laughing. Som. sees hat. Arguing adlib.) Str. tells Com. and they start to tell it to the other Com. and exit. (Enter other Com. starts to tell it to 2nd Com., getting it all bawled up. 2nd Com. switches hats. (1st Com. takes hat off 2nd Com. head and starts jumping and laughs. 2nd Com. asks him what he is laughing at. 1st Com. shows him hat.) Says, I was jumping on your hat. 2nd Com. says that ain't my hat, it's yours. (1st Com. chases him off.)"

In contrast, some bits were simply a series of brief, unrelated jokes, presented by a pair of performers. These comedy dialogues, often called "sidewalk conversations" or "sidewalk patter," appeared in many gag books. A "sidewalk conversation" was ordinarily nothing more than a couple of dozen two- or three-line jokes designed to be presented by "He and She" or "Pat and Mike" or "Comic and Straight." An old advertisement defines it as "a string of funny questions and funny answers intended to be 'done' in quick succession." One such sidewalk conversation taken from a gagbook called "McNally's Bulletin" is presented here. As with many of the other acts in this anthology, it is unlikely that most professional performers used the material intact. Instead, they undoubtedly reshaped the gags to suit their own stock character, time limitations, and the like, dropping some of the jokes and adding favorite pieces of material from other sources.

The two minstrel "cross-fires" that follow extend somewhat the simple premise of a string of unrelated jokes told by Comic and Straight. Here the traditional minstrel Middleman or Interlocutor serves as the Straight, while the two Endmen, Tambo and Bones, offer up comedy lines at his expense. In both cross-fires there is at least a touch of theme, to the extent that most of the jokes are not strictly random, but are more or less related to a unifying idea. The "Messrs. Grin and Barrett" bit adopts the crossfire idea to a pair of Irish comics.

Dale and Lois Madden's tent show act is essentially an extended dialogue. The act, recorded at the 1981 Smithsonian Folklife Festival, begins as an Interruption scene in which the Straight never finishes her song because of the onslaught of jokes from the Comic. Gradually it shifts to a brief two-character "schoolroom" scene, not unlike the more developed schoolroom sketch found in the next section. The comic in this act, by the way, was dressed as the traditional Toby character often seen in tent show plays, complete with painted freckles, red "fright" wig, and baggy pants.

A third minstrel piece, "A Pack of Cards and the Bible," adapts the traditional "deck of cards" routine for Tambo and Bones. Like the monologue version found earlier in this anthology, it tells an essentially complete story. In doing so it moves in the direction of a fully developed "bit."

Often the bit is built around the dramatization of a single joke. "Buzzin' the Bee'' and ''Niagara Falls,'' for example, are classic bits which are fundamentally nothing more than practical jokes presented in dialogue form. By the same token, ''Three Times Three are Ten'' is merely a mathematical brain-teaser split up between the Straight, the Comic and the Second Comedian. ''Izzy-Wuzzy,'' which is simply a piece of elaborate word play in dialogue form, resembles in many ways the famous Abbott and Costello ''Who's on First'' bit.

''Prickly Heat,'' a doctor bit from burlesque, is another classic in which a slightly risque joke is split up among four characters. There is a hint of setting and properties in the Chuck Callahan version, but virtually no plot as such. Like several other bits, ''Prickly Heat'' has a ''blackout'' ending in which—theoretically, at least—the stage is to be plunged into darkness as the final punch line is delivered.

Bob Noell's medicine show version of ''The Photograph Gallery'' bit develops plot somewhat more through the device of a naive character, Jake, who is supposed to be sitting for his photograph. Much of the bit, however, is made up of Jake's gratuitous clowning, which bears only a formal relationship to the slender plot. The blackface character of Jake, found in many medicine show bits and sketches, suggests the shows' strong ties to the minstrel tradition. The burlesque bit which follows, ''The Bull Fight,'' moves somewhat farther in the direction of a full-fledged sketch because of its use of properties, sound effects, and even a crowd of extras. Yet ''The Bull Fight'' remains little more than an elaborate verbal sparring match between Comic and Straight.

SIDEWALK CONVERSATIONS
FOR MALE AND FEMALE

He: Why does a chicken cross the road?
She: I don't know. I'm only the farmer's daughter.

He: Every time I kiss you I feel like a hundred dollars.
She: Well, don't try to become a millionaire in one night.

She: My fiance lost all his money in Wall Street.
He: I suppose you feel sorry for him?
She: Yes, he'll miss me.

He: Time seems to stand still when I'm with a clever girl like you.
She: Well, no wonder. You've a face that would stop any clock.

He: Isn't it terrible how many girls are shooting their husbands nowadays?
She: Yes, it isn't nearly as good publicity as it used to be.

He: My wife had ten men after her until she married me.
She: That must make you feel proud.
He: No, they were bill collectors and now they're after me.

He: Give me a little kiss.
She: No, I'm saving my kisses for the MEN I marry.

She: Do you attend a place of worship?
He: Yes, I do. In fact, I'm on my way to see her now.

He: Does your husband ever take your little hand in his?
She: Yes, and twists it until I drop the gun.

She: That was a slave bracelet you gave me, wasn't it darling?
He: Yes. I had to SLAVE five months to get the money to buy it.

She: What do you do when you get tired of a girl's empty conversation?
He: I give in and take her to a restaurant.

He: I only say what I know.
She: Ah, one of those big, strong, SILENT men.

She: I'm in favor of some rough-house.
He: I second the commotion.

She: My husband once made a quart of whiskey last from one year to another.
He: How did he do that?
She: He started drinking it at five minutes to twelve on the nite of December
    31st.

He: I'm happy because I've just killed a saxophone player.
She: Good heavens, what will you get?
He: Sleep.

She: I'd like to get married. Do you think any fellow would be my husband?
He: Don't ask me.

She: Did you hear about that lady aviator who established a new endurance
    record?
He: No; how long did she talk?

He: If I had a million dollars do you know where I'd be?
She: Yes, you'd be on our honeymoon.

She: I met a man last night who can read a person's character by the face.
He: Did you try him out?
She: Yes, and was my face READ?

She: You want to marry a girl who comes from a good family, don't you?
He: Yes, and the further she comes from it the better.

She: When I bake my cakes they are all made with three quarters ingredients and one quarter luck.
He: Yeah, HARD LUCK.

He: I wonder what's the height of dumbness.
She: About six feet, aren't you?

She: I hear that your friend John went into marriage with his eyes shut.
He: Yes, his wife's father packs an awful wallop.

She: On a stormy night don't you get tired of hearing the everlasting pitter patter?
He: Yes, it never rains but it bores.

He: I had to quit dancing last night.
She: Corn?
He: No, rye.

He: Darling, I've lost my entire fortune to a slick oil promoter. What have I to offer you now?
She: Give me his address.

He: You're an awfully sweet kid, darling, and now that we're married promise me you won't change.
She: Aw, darling, you'll let me be a blonde just once in a while, won't you?

He: That girl I was with at the masquerade ball admits she's thirty-five years old.
She: Aren't you ashamed to be going around with a FIFTY-year-old woman?

She: Did you read in the paper about Jones running over his mother-in-law?
He: No, I seldom read the sporting pages.

He: You can get all sorts of things from kissing.
She: Yes, fur coats, diamonds, roadsters and everything.

She: Will you love me when my hair is gray?
He: Why not? Haven't I stuck with you through brown, black, red and blonde?

She: Our engagement is ended! And don't you dare ask me to return your ring.
He: I won't but the installment house I bought it from probably will.

He: My father's a real patriot.
She: How can you prove he's a real patriot?
He: He whistles the "Star Spangled Banner" while he makes out his income tax report.

He: Do you use Palmolive soap?
She: No.
He: Then, have you a little fairy in your home?
She: No, but I have a fairy's wand—wand to give me a fur coat?

She: I think kissing is childish.
He: So do I, baby.

He: Why should we stop all social activities during Lent?
She: Because our Winter clothes are worn out and our Summer clothes are not yet ready.

He: What would you say to a little kiss?
She: Stingy.

He: If you want me to teach you golf, I'll have to talk to you just like a brother.
She: Oh, no you won't! I'll not stand for any of your cussing.

He: How did your sister ever decide to dye her hair red?
She: Oh, she just told the beauty operator that *henna* color would do.

He: I suppose lots of things I say make you feel as if you could beat my brains out.
She: No, everything you say makes me realize there aren't any there to beat out.

She: When we get married we won't be like John and his wife. They're always knocking each other.
He: What about?
She: The room.

She: Believe me. I cursed the day I was born.
He: That's strange. I didn't curse till I was a year old.

She: When you keep on kissing me, it makes me tremble from head to foot.
He: Yes, and when you tremble from head to foot, it makes me keep on kissing you.

He: You say your husband writes you from New York that he wants to hang himself?
She: Yes, let's hurry to the telegraph office. I want to send him a WIRE.

He: Don't forget it; knowledge is power.
She: More power to you.

She: I read where a man ate twenty pounds of sausage in ten minutes. What would you call that? A record?
He: No, baloney!

He: I tell you, I always act like a gentleman when I'm full of liquor.
She: Then hurry up and get drunk.

She: Our friendship ripened quickly, didn't it?
He: Yes, we got to know each other in the wink of an eye.

She: Say, you're looking fine. You must have had your daily dozen today.
He: No, so far I've only drunk six.

He: The man you refused to marry last night has jumped from the thirteenth floor.
She: Heavens! Didn't he know that would be unlucky?

She: Do you think smoking is a good thing for a woman with a voice like mine?
He: Yes, you don't sing when you're smoking.

REMARKABLE BRAVERY
CROSS-FIRE

MIDDLE: I understand you attended the banquet the other night. Did you enjoy yourself? Did you *take* well?

BONES: You bet I did; I got three spoons, four napkin-rings and a sugarbowl. I would have *swiped more* if I'd had a chance.

TAMBO: (*Interrupting, to Middleman.*) Say! Does your sister use face powder?

MID: She uses a *little* powder, I think.

TAMBO: A *little?* She puts it on so thick that she ought to join the plasterers' union. Oh! *what* a face she has—and wrinkles! Ugh! They are good for the flies to hide in.

MID: I hope you will not criticize my sister's features.

BONES: Her feet! Oh! (*Laughs.*) She'd be awful tall if there wasn't so *much* of her on the ground. Feet! Oh! They are like a couple of trunks.

TAMBO: I guess she must leave her feet outside of the room when she retires at night, doesn't she?

MID: You wouldn't believe she wears number twos?

BONES: You mean *twenty-twos!*

TAMBO: *Two hundred and twenty-twos!*

MID: Now, there is a brave and noble girl. Let me relate an incident. The other night a burglar entered the house and began, dark lantern in hand, to search—

BONES: For her feet? Why he couldn't help *falling* over them.

MID: (*Annoyed.*) No! No! While the burglar was searching, my sister heard him.

TAMBO: He stepped on her feet, and next day she felt it.

MID: Oh, listen! She heard the burglar—what did she do?

BOTH: *Stepped on him* and he died!

MID: No; she didn't scream nor betray timidity, but ran out—

BOTH: (*Angry.*) Yes, yes.

TAMBO: I don't see how she could run.

BONES: May be somebody *carried her feet in a wheelbarrow* and she followed them.

MID: No! I tell you! I repeat she ran—

BOTH: And tumbled over them.

MID: No, sir! She ran to the corner and found a policeman—

BONES: Fast asleep on her feet?

MID: (*Very angry.*) No!

TAMBO: Then he was inside one of her shoes?

MID: No! She found the policeman, brought him back to the house—

BOTH: *And he arrested her feet!*

MID: (*Rises in anger.*) Shut up!

BONES: Shut up, yourself! They weren't *your* feet, were they?

TAMBO: Shut up your sister's *Trilbys.*

MID: (*Excited.*) The policeman came to the house and arrested the burglar. That's what I call *bravery*!

TAMBO: Get out! *Any* girl in this town could do *that*.

BONES: Certainly they could if they had the *chance*, but they couldn't *get* the chance.

TAMBO: No; she'd *never* get a chance.

MID: Why not?

BOTH: She *couldn't find a policeman*.

STUPIDITY AND SOLDIERS
CROSS-FIRE

MIDDLE: What were you doing to-day capering in the middle of the street like a lunatic?

BONES: Trying to dodge a cross-eyed girl who was on a bike.

TAMBO: Say! How did you like the shot you got to-day?

MID: What do you mean?

TAMBO: (*Talking to Bones.*) He tried to be fresh and he says to a young lady passing by: "Sissy, does your mother know you're out!" The girl says: "Oh, yes! And she gave me a penny to buy a monkey. *Are you for sale?*" (*Laughs.*)

BONES: Speaking of money. You know how mean he is. (*Referring to Mid.*) Well, he swallowed an old-fashioned copper cent by mistake (*laughs*), and the doctor made him cough up *two dollars*.

TAMBO: Show you how smart he thinks he is. (*Meaning Mid.*) I met him at the depot and he was chuckling to himself. I says: What pleases you? He says: I've got the best of the railroad company this time. I've bought a return ticket and I'm not going to use it.

MID: (*Angry.*) Oh, gentlemen, I'm not so stupid as all that!

BONES: You're worse! He's so mean that he never goes to a barber to have his hair cut. He waits until winter time and sticks his head into a bucket of water and lets his hair freeze stiff; then he *breaks it off*.

TAMBO: Then he got a job in a dry goods store as clerk. A lady came in and made him take down seventy bolts of silks and satins. Then she says: I don't think I'll purchase anything; I was merely *looking* for a friend. He says: If you think your friend is *in the other bolts* I'll take them down, too. But he's a chump!

BONES: I've got to tell this one on him. He was eating his dinner at the hotel and the waiter placed a finger-bowl beside him. He looked at it, picked it up and drank half of its contents. Then he turned to me and says: *That's the thinnest lemonade I ever tasted.*

MID: (*Pleadingly.*) Oh, gentlemen! Please do not hold me up to ridicule in this manner.

TAMBO: Oh! You frozen piece of pie! He went to the butcher's and asked him for ten cents worth of liver; and he says: Don't give me any *liver with bones in it.* (*Laughs.*) He ought to work in a livery stable!

BONES: And he wanted to enlist in the army. The officer says: Which branch of the service do you prefer? Army or Navy? He says: Both. Officer says: Which regiment? He says: Put me in the Seventh regiment. I've got a brother in the Sixth regiment and *I want to be near him.*

MID: (*Stamping foot.*) All this is nonsense! Now tell me who makes the best soldiers for Uncle Sam?

TAMBO: Auburn haired soldiers, for they are always *Reddy.*

BONES: Pawnbrokers make the best soldiers. They can send *Three Balls* to the enemy. No, sir; Nigger soldiers are the best of all.

MID: Why?

BONES: They are *fast colors* and *never run.*

MESSRS. GRIN & BARRETT

(*Open with song. Grin after finish of song still continues to sing.*)

BARRETT: That'll do! That'll do! We're through singing!

(*Grin still sings.*)

BARRETT: I say! I said that'll do!

GRIN: O, you said that, did ye?

BARRETT: I did.

GRIN: Well, it's me own song I'm singing.

BARRETT: Doesn't make any difference. Stop it!

GRIN: O, I thought there was another verse.

BARRETT: No, sir; that is all.

(*Grin starts to leave stage.*)

BARRETT: Hold on, Mike! Where ye goin'?

GRIN: You said that was all.

BARRETT: Well, I'll be a-tellin' ye when to leave the stage.

GRIN: O, and how long have ye been manager of the troupe?

BARRETT: I'm not the manager.

GRIN: Well, any time you get to be manager I'll enlist in the army again.

BARRETT: In the army? And when was ye in the army?

GRIN: O, I'm a vet.

BARRETT: And did ye be after holdin' any dangerous position in the army?

GRIN: Sure. I held the most dangerous position in the whole army.

BARRETT: And what was that?

GRIN: I had charge of the sixteen mules.

BARRETT: B'gorry! That was a snap.

GRIN: I guess you don't know what army mules are. There's sixteen feet on each leg.

BARRETT: Is that so?

GRIN: Yis, and they're always workin'.

BARRETT: It do be like the rapid-fire idea.

GRIN: Yis; and the devils use smokeless powder, too. B'gorry! I'll never forget the day I sailed away and left me sweetheart to go to the Philicubas.

BARRETT: Hold on, Mike! You mean the Porto-phillies.

GRIN: Yis, the Santi-ricos. I went to San Transport and took a Francisco.

BARRETT: Why didn't you go to New York, and take a Manhattan?

GRIN: For the same reason I didn't go to the Catskills and take a Pousse Cafe.

BARRETT: All right, Mike; I'll let ye tell it.

GRIN: Well, as I said before: I'll never forget the partin' from me sweetheart, Bridget. She threw her arms about me neck and says: "Mike, me darlin', be a brave boy, do your duty and come back to me full of *holes* for the future, and—"

BARRETT: (*Interrupting.*) Hold on, Mike! Did she say she wanted you full of holes?

GRIN: Who said anything about holes?

BARRETT: You said Bridget wanted you shot full of holes.

GRIN: Nothin' of the kind! I said "full of hope for the future."

BARRETT: O, yes—shot full of soap for the future. Go ahead.

GRIN: Well, the ship was three days out, and we had to make port again.

BARRETT: B'gorry! You must have been a thirsty lot of soldiers.

GRIN: Did I mention anything about bein' thirsty?

BARRETT: You said they had to make port again. I suppose the water was bad.

GRIN: Yis, I did say port. Port is a nautical term for a sea-coast town—a wharf —the place from where we started from, see!

BARRETT: O, yis. What was the matter? Did the captain forget where he was goin'?

GRIN: No, ye Irish lobster! We had spiral meningitis aboard.

BARRETT: And he didn't have a ticket?

GRIN: Who didn't have a ticket?

BARRETT: Why, that Spaniard you spoke of.

GRIN: I never said a word about a Spaniard.

BARRETT: Well, what nationality was he, then?

GRIN: Was who?

BARRETT: Spinal men-he-cheat-us.

GRIN: O, me boy, yer ignorance is to be puttyed. It was a sickness we had on the ship. Do ye understand?

BARRETT: O, yis. I had one of them gags meself once.

GRIN: And what was it?

BARRETT: I'm thinkin' it was croup, but I dunno.

GRIN: Well, as I was sayin', Bridget threw her arms around me neck, and—

BARRETT: (*Interrupting.*) And landed with her right.

GRIN: No, no—nothin' of the kind.

BARRETT: O, then hittin' in clinches was barred.

GRIN: Of course; say, am I a-tellin' of this?

BARRETT: From the bottom of me vest I'll believe ye. Go ahead!

GRIN: As I was a sayin', Bridget threw—

BARRETT: (*Interrupting.*) B'gorry! I wouldn't have stood for it.

GRIN: Stood for what?

BARRETT: Bridget throwin' things at me.

GRIN: As a decent man I ask ye once more to let me tell this.

BARRETT: Well, I'll forgive ye. Go ahead!

GRIN: Just as I was a kissin' of her good-by, the conductor hollered, "All a-board!" sharp like, and—

BARRETT: Hold on! hold on! What did they want with a conductor on a ship?

GRIN: And who said anything about a conductor?

BARRETT: You said the conductor yelled for everybody to get aboard ship.

GRIN: I never said a word about a ship. Yer crazy, man. I'm askin' again to let me tell me story.

BARRETT: Well, go ahead!

GRIN: Just as the ship left the wharf, the conductor says to the motorman, "I think there's a leak in the balloon," and just—

BARRETT: And now will ye hold up a bit?

GRIN: So yer stoppin' me again, are ye?

BARRETT: Yis, ye was gattin' all twisted. Talkin' about the motorman, and the balloon, and the—

GRIN: I never said a word about a balloon. What's the matter with ye, anyway?

BARRETT: I'll let ye alone. Go on and lie.

GRIN: Well, don't interrupt me agin. You see, me boy, I never was in a coal mine before in the whole course of me life, and when the elevator started down I yelled to the barkeep to fill up the glasses agin, and—

BARRETT: Mike! Mike! Where are ye now?

GRIN: Man alive! are ye goin' to let me tell this, and not keep cuttin' in all the time?

BARRETT: I'd like to, but, b'gorry! yer in a balloon one minute, the next in a trolley-car, then in a coal-mine, and now yer in a saloon.

GRIN: I am?

BARRETT: Yis, ye was a minute ago.

GRIN: Was ye with me?

BARRETT: Sure; I've been with ye right along.

GRIN: Are ye sober?

BARRETT: Of course I am.

GRIN: Am I sober?

BARRETT: I think ye are.

GRIN: Then, it's plain to be seen, Mr. Barrett, that we never was in a saloon. Now don't stop me again. As I was sayin'—

BARRETT: Do ye know much about sheep?

GRIN: Sheep?

BARRETT: That's what I mentioned—sheep.

GRIN: B'gorry! I had the finest piece of roast mutton last night that ye ever laid yer eyes on.

BARRETT: I do be speakin' now of live sheep.

GRIN: O, live sheep! Why, me boy, I was raised with sheep; I know all about them.

BARRETT: Then can ye be after tellin' me what kind of sheep eat the most, the white sheep or the black sheep?

GRIN: B'gorry! I'm thinking ye have me stuck.

BARRETT: Why, the white sheep eat the most, of course.

GRIN: And why of course?

BARRETT: Because there are more white sheep than black sheep.

GRIN: My! O, my! but there's a smart boy for ye. Well, to go on with me story: The minute I got in that automobile I knew there was goin' to be trouble. I pulled the—

BARRETT: Mike, stop a bit, ye must be dry. (*Goes to wing and gets tin pail.*) Take this and go get a pint of beer.

GRIN: (*Takes pail.*) It's a foine fellow ye are. Give me the price and I'll be after it and back agin in a jiffy.

BARRETT: Tut, tut, me boy! But to get beer without the price—that's the trick.

GRIN: (*Scratching his head.*) And it's a purty good trick, too. (*Exits with can—re-enters quickly hands can to Barrett.*) There ye are, me boy! Drink hearty!

BARRETT: (*Takes can—looks inside.*) Why, how can I drink when there is no beer in it?

GRIN: Me boy, to drink out of a can when there is beer in it, anybody can do; but to drink beer out of a can when there is no beer—that's a trick.

BARRETT: And it's a purty good trick, too.

GRIN: I guess that will embrace ye for a period. Well, the horse hadn't gone more than forty feet before—

BARRETT: Mike, and what's yer father doin'?

GRIN: Oh, he's rushed to death.

BARRETT: Is yer father a man of means, Mike?

GRIN: I should say so! Everybody says he's the meanest man in town.

BARRETT: Where are ye stoppin' now?

GRIN: I'm puttin' up at the Hotel Sooner.

BARRETT: Hotel Sooner? And why do they call it that?

GRIN: Because you'd sooner stay up all night than go to bed.

BARRETT: What's the matter with the beds?

GRIN: The beds are all right, but the bugs, me boy—the bugs are awful bad.

BARRETT: O, I wouldn't care about the bugs.

GRIN: I don't mind the bugs.

BARRETT: Then what's eatin' ye?

GRIN: Well, the fact is I haven't got the blood to spare.

BARRETT: O, that's too thin!

GRIN: No; it's me that's too thin. Well, as I was sayin', the bicycle struck me and—

BARRETT: What's the best way to make gloves wear twice as long?

GRIN: Wear white ones because there more of them.

BARRETT: I'm now speakin' of gloves—not sheep.

GRIN: And yer askin' me what's the best way to make gloves wear twice as long?

BARRETT: That's the question I propounded.

GRIN: What color?

BARRETT: Any color.

GRIN: Then I don't know.

BARRETT: Wear one at a time.

GRIN: Stop yer gaggin' and let me finish me story.

BARRETT: Go ahead! I hope ye choke!

GRIN: The same to ye and many of them. As I was sayin'

BARRETT: By the way, what's that mark on yer face?

GRIN: That's a berth-mark.

BARRETT: A berth-mark? I never saw it before.

GRIN: That's a berth-mark all right. You see, I was going to Omaha the other night and I got into the wrong berth.

BARRETT: Serves ye right.

GRIN: As I was sayin'

BARRETT: Can ye tell me the three quickest methods of communication?

GRIN: I don't know about three; one is to fall on a sidewalk after slippin' on a banana-peel.

BARRETT: That may be one, but I'm speakin' of three.

GRIN: Tell me.

BARRETT: The three quickest methods of communication are the telegraph, telephone and tell a woman.

GRIN: That's true. I was in the crazy house yesterday on a visit.

BARRETT: How are they over there?

GRIN: Oh, just crazy to get out. While I was there I noticed the clock in the hall; it was an hour slow. I says to one of the crazy guys: "What's the matter with that clock? It isn't right." He says: I know it. If it was it wouldn't be in here."

BARRETT: Are ye goin' to tell me about that trip to the "Phillicubas?"
GRIN: I've gone there and got back agin.
BARRETT: And now where ye goin'?
GRIN: You come with me. I know where they have them high, cold and wet.
BARRETT: Well, as I was sayin', that's about all.

(*Finish with specialties.*)

INTERRUPTION SCENE

SUZIE: (*Singing.*) Somewhere . . .
TOBY: (*Creates confusion in the audience.*) Hurry up, the show's gonna start pretty soon.
SUZIE: (*Singing.*) Somewhere a voice . . .
(*Toby creates more ruckus.*)
SUZIE: Just a moment, just a moment young man, just a moment young man, you're disturbing me.
TOBY: When's your show gonna start?
SUZIE: Oh, it's already started.
TOBY: Are you gonna be in the show?
SUZIE: Well, I'm a very small part of it, but at least the show has started.
TOBY: (*Speaks softly.*) Well, I want my money back.
SUZIE: Oh, young man. Haven't you got a seat?
TOBY: Ya, I got a seat, but I got no place to put it.
SUZIE: Oh! You find a seat and be quiet or we're gonna have you escorted out. I'm supposed to sing a song here you know.
TOBY: What's the name of the song you're singing?
SUZIE: "Somewhere a Voice is Calling."
TOBY: Ha, that ain't what this man here said it was. (*Points to spectator.*)
SUZIE: What'd he say it was?
TOBY: "Somewhere a Cow is Bawling."
SUZIE: That isn't nice and he didn't say that either. And I think that's right down mean of you. You know I'm being paid to sing this song.
TOBY: You mean to tell me that the people here at the folklife festival pay you?
SUZIE: Oh, you bet.
TOBY: How much do they pay you?
SUZIE: Fifty dollars a performance.
TOBY: Oh!
SUZIE: That's so.
TOBY: Hey, lady, do you know the difference between you and the man that dyes the wool on a sheep?
SUZIE: No, what is the difference?

TOBY: Well, that fellow is a lamb dyer; you're a . . . (*Suzie interrupts.*)

SUZIE: Toby, that isn't very nice of you, I think that's very very mean of you. You know, this is the way I make my living. I want you to know that I have six starving children at home, and I have to work very hard trying to keep the wolf away from the door.

TOBY: Keep the wolf away from the door? He's been down to our house and had pups!

SUZIE: Oh, come up here, young man.

TOBY: It's all off, it's all off.

SUZIE: What's all off?

TOBY: (*Points to a bald man in the audience.*) The hair on that man's head.

SUZIE: Hey you, hey, hey, you've caused enough disturbance, now I'd just like to get a chance to look at your face; come up on stage. (*Toby obliges.*) As I live and breathe this is Toby we have here.

TOBY: Yep, that's me.

SUZIE: Where have you been?

TOBY: I been over to school.

SUZIE: School?

TOBY: Yes.

SUZIE: Don't give me that.

TOBY: Us kids go to a special school during festival week.

SUZIE: Well, I'm going to say it would have to be special because school is out.

TOBY: Yeh, but we go to school just the same all the time.

SUZIE: Isn't that remarkable? You know it isn't every day you find a man your age who wants to go back to school, you know?

TOBY: I've always said you can't get enough edu-ma-cation.

SUZIE: Oh, isn't that remarkable? What all do you take?

TOBY: Last week I got two lead pencils, and a book, and I got three pairs of . . . What's the matter?

SUZIE: Who said anything about what you steal? I mean what subjects.

TOBY: Oh, readin', and writin', and 'rithmetic, geography and all them things.

SUZIE: Isn't that great?

TOBY: Yes, we have them all.

SUZIE: (*Interrupting him.*) How are you in arithmetic?

TOBY: Awful good in arithmetic. Best in my class.

SUZIE: Are you really? How many are in your class?

TOBY: Just me and the teacher.

SUZIE: That's what I figured.

TOBY: But we're awful good, you know.

SUZIE: I bet I could give you a problem you couldn't handle.

TOBY: You can't fool me.

SUZIE: Let me give you a problem. If I had two apples, four bananas, two peaches, and one pear, and I were to give them to you, and you were to eat them—quick, quick, quick—what would you have?

TOBY: A bellyache!

SUZIE: Now, how are you in English?

TOBY: Well, you see, I'm not English, I'm Irish.

SUZIE: I don't give a hoot about your nationality, I didn't ask you your nationality.

TOBY: What do you mean nationality? You gotta quit using them big words.

SUZIE: Don't you know anything?

TOBY: No, no, what is nationality?

SUZIE: Nationality, Toby, means wherever you're born, that's what it makes you.

TOBY: Wherever you're born that's what it makes you?

SUZIE: That's right. For instance, if you were born in Scotland, you'd be Scottish.

TOBY: If you're born in Scotland you'd be Scottish. That's right.

SUZIE: Born in Ireland, be Irish.

TOBY: That's easy, born in Ireland, be Irish.

SUZIE: Born in France, you'd be a Frenchman.

TOBY: Born in France, you'd be a Frenchman.

SUZIE: (*Interrupting him.*) It's that simple. Wherever you're born, that's what it makes you.

TOBY: If you was born in bed, you'd be a bedbug.

SUZIE: That's right. (*Audience laughs.*) NO! No, no, no. Come here, Toby.

TOBY: Heh. She sounds like a propaganda machine, don't she?

SUZIE: A what?

TOBY: Propaganda . . .

SUZIE: Now there you go, there you go. I bet you a penny you don't know the meaning of the word propaganda. There he goes using those . . .

TOBY: (*Interrupting her.*) You've done lost your penny. I know what the meaning of the word propaganda is.

SUZIE: Do you?

TOBY: You remember the day behind yesterday? You was out at our house and seen all the pigs.

SUZIE: Oh, you bet.

TOBY: See all the little piglets? And all the cows? All the little cowlets? And horses? All the little horselets? Did you see all the geese?

SUZIE: (*She answers "yes" after all his questions.*) Oh, you had a nice flock of geese.

TOBY: But you didn't see no little gooslets runnin' around, did ya?

SUZIE: Come to think of it, I didn't see a solitary one.

TOBY: Right, there's the meaning of the word, right there.

SUZIE: What do you mean, right there's the meaning of the word?

TOBY: We didn't have the propaganda.

SUZIE: Toby, come here.

TOBY: Would you like a little more time on that? (*To audience.*)

SUZIE: Toby, come here. Toby, in your English class, did your teacher ever select a word and real quick-like have the children make a sentence using that word?

TOBY: Oh, yes, lots of times.

SUZIE: Can you do that?

TOBY: Yeah!

SUZIE: Make me a nice long sentence, a nice one now, a nice sentence using the word . . . let me see . . .

TOBY: Let me have a look too.

SUZIE: . . . ransom in it.

TOBY: Ransom!

SUZIE: Yes.

TOBY: A tomcat sat on the sewing machine. He was so tall and handsome. The machine ran nine stitches up his tail. And you bet the doggone cat ran some.

SUZIE: That wasn't the right kind of ransom. Make me a nice long sentence very quickly with the word diadem.

TOBY: Diadem. Those who drink moonshine diadem sight quicker than those who don't.

SUZIE: Ooh! Now, did you have poetry in your class?

TOBY: Yeah, we had poetry; the teacher writes the poetry up on the blackboard.

SUZIE: Well, perhaps your teacher would make up two lines and ask the children to make up two lines.

TOBY: Yep.

SUZIE: To rhyme with her two?

TOBY: Yep.

SUZIE: To make a little poem?

TOBY: To make a poem.

SUZIE: Can you do that?

TOBY: Oh, I can do that, yep.

SUZIE: Well, I don't care what you do, but I want it to be nice and clean; we have a mixed audience out here.

TOBY: We got a nice looking group of people.

SUZIE: Oh, a mighty fine looking people. Just, just look over here, Toby. I want you to know that I have the cream of society on my side. (*Gestures.*)

TOBY: Over here, huh?

SUZIE: This is the *cream* of society. (*Gestures.*)

TOBY: (*Laughing.*) The cream of society. I guess I've got the skim milk . . .

SUZIE: Oh! Look, look Toby, look at all those little dears out there.

TOBY: Yeah, well I got a few old bucks over here. (*Gestures.*)

SUZIE: Oh, get back here and do your poem. Come on, you can't take all day. Do me a nice little poem now. I'll make up two lines, you try to make up two lines to rhyme.

TOBY: Go ahead.

SUZIE: I'm gonna try and catch ya.

TOBY: Go ahead, try to catch me.

SUZIE: OK. Old Mother Hubbard went to the cupboard.
To get her poor daughter a dress . . .

TOBY: . . . And when she got there the cupboard was bare,
And so was her daughter I guess.

SUZIE: That was awful.

TOBY: You said it had to rhyme.

SUZIE: The boy stood on the burning deck,
His baggage was checked for Jerusalem . . .

TOBY: The boy stood on the burning . . . Jerusalem, huh?

SUZIE: Uh huh.

TOBY: You think you're smart don't ya? There's no word that'll rhyme with Jerusalem.

SUZIE: Oh, there's lots of words. I can't help it 'cause you're a dumbhead.

TOBY: There's no word . . .

SUZIE: (*Interrupting him.*) I'll try you once more.
The boy stood on the burning deck,
His baggage was checked for Jerusalem . . .

TOBY: His heels went up and his head went down,
And he busted his almagusalem.

SUZIE: That wasn't funny, Toby. You know any other poems, I mean all by yourself?

TOBY: I know a poem about Nellie.

SUZIE: Do you? Give me one right quick. Nice now. And it must rhyme.

TOBY: I once knew a girl by the name of Nellie,
She stepped in a mudhole up to her . . . (*Points to Suzie's ankle.*)

SUZIE: Toby! Toby! You just watch it, young man. Anyway, that didn't rhyme.

TOBY: The mudhole wasn't deep enough!

SUZIE: OK, that's enough out of you.

TOBY: Raise up your hands, touch your toes,
And I'll show you where the wild goose goes. (*Gesture.*)

SUZIE: Toby Hopkinson, I'm not gonna give you another chance, one more mistake and I'll box your ears.

TOBY: I wish I were a little fish, all froze up in the ice,
And when the pretty girls go skatin' by,
Oh, Lord, wouldn't that be nice.

(*Suzie does a fake slap and exits.*)

A PACK OF CARDS AND THE BIBLE

END: Say, Sam, did you know I was a soldier in the last war?

INT: No. Is that so?

END: Yes, sir. I fit and bled for my country. I was took prisoner once, too.

INT: Well, tell us all about it, Tambo.

END: Well, you see, Sam, the chaplain of our regiment commanded us always to attend church Sundays. Well, all the soldiers but me had a Bible, or Prayer Book, or something; and when church began they all took them out and commenced to read. I didn't have anything but a pack of cards, so I pulled them out of my pocket and commenced to look them over—

INT: That was very wrong, Tambo. The idea of taking a deck of cards out in church!

END: That's what the sergeant of the company said. And when church was over he had me arrested and took me before the judge. But the judge didn't do anything to me. He let me off, for I convinced him that my intentions were all right.

INT: How did you do that, Tambo?

END: Why, I spread the cards before His Honor, and said, Do you see these cards, judge? They serve me for a Bible and almanac and Common Prayer Book. When I see the ace, it reminds me there is but one God; when I see the deuce, it reminds me of the Father and Son; when I see the trey, it reminds me of the Father, Son and Holy Ghost; when I see the four, it reminds me of the four evangelists that preached—Matthew, Mark, Luke, and John; when I see the five, it reminds me of the five wise virgins that trimmed their lamps.

INT: So far, so good, Tambo. Let's have more.

END: When I see the six, it reminds me that in six days the Lord made heaven and earth; when I see the seven, it reminds me that God rested on the seventh day after his great work. When I see the eight, it reminds me of the eight righteous people that were saved when the flood came— Noah and his wife, their three children, and their wives. The children, of course, were their sons. And when I see the nine, it reminds me of the nine lepers that were healed by the Savior. There were nine out of ten that never returned thanks. And when I see the ten, I'm reminded of the Ten Commandments; when I see the king, it reminds me of the Great King of Heaven; the queen reminds me of the Queen of Sheba, who visited Solomon.

INT: Well, Tambo, you've described every card in the pack but one.

END: What's that?

INT: The knave, better known as the jack.

END: Well, the knave reminds me of the fellow that arrested me.

INT: You proved pretty conclusively that a pack of cards could be a substitute for the Bible and the Common Prayer Book, but I do not see where you make it serve for an almanac.

END: Well, when I count the spots in a pack of cards, I find exactly three hundred and sixty-five, as many as there are days in a year. When I count the cards, I find fifty-two, the number of weeks in a year. I find there are twelve picture cards in the pack, representing the twelve months in a year; and on counting the tricks, I find thirteen, the number of weeks in a quarter. So you see, Sam, a little pack of sinful-looking playing cards serves me for a Bible, a Prayer Book, and an almanac!

BUZZIN' THE BEE

STR: (*Enters.*) There's a certain guy round here that thinks he's pretty wise. I've got a little game here that I just thought of, and I think I'll try it out on him and get a good laugh. (*Hears Chuck off S.*)

CHUCK: (*Enters.*)

STR: Hello, Chuckie. You're just the boy I'm looking for.

CHUCK: I ain't got a dime.

STR: Now listen Chuck. I just figured out a new game. It's called Buzzin' the Bee. Chuck, it's one of the funniest games you ever heard of.

CHUCK: Bum the buzzle bee?

STR: No. No. Buzzing the Bumble Bee.

CHUCK: Nope. Never heard of that game before.

STR: Why, of course you didn't. I just figured it out myself. Chuck, will you laugh. (*Laughs.*) You'll laugh like you never laughed before.

CHUCK: Well, I want to laugh. I ain't laughed since Paw kicked Maw in the stomach. I'd like to play that game.

STR: Alright. Now I'll explain it to you. Now, listen very carefully. Now you know that every bee hive has a queen bee. And also a king bee. Well, the queen bee stays home all day, and never has to do any work. The king goes out and gathers the honey. When he comes home at night with the honey, he knocks at the door. And the queen bee comes out and says, "Give it to me."

CHUCK: Oh, you've got to have a king bee and a queen bee?

STR: Oh, yes: you've got to have a king bee and a queen bee.

CHUCK: Well, how are we going to play the game?

STR: I'll explain it. I'll be the king bee. I go out and buzz from flower to flower and gather the honey. Now you . . .

CHUCK: Here's where I come in.

STR: You're going to be the queen bee.

CHUCK: Here's where I go out. (*Bus.*) Queen bee? What do I have to do?

STR: The queen bee, all she has to do . . .

CHUCK: Oh, oh. I can't play that game.

STR: Why not?

CHUCK: I can't be no she.

STR: Why can't you be a she?

CHUCK: Huh. It's too late. (*Strts to ex.*)

STR: No, no Chuck. This is just a game. The reason I want you to be the queen bee is, you don't have to do any work.

CHUCK: No work? I like that job. I'll play.

STR: Alright. Now you see that room over there. (*Points L.*)

CHUCK: Sure.

STR: Well, that is the blue room.

CHUCK: Ah, the blueing room.

STR: No. The blue room. Now in that room there are a lot of honey bees.

CHUCK: Honey bees in that room?

STR: That's right. Oh, by the way Chuck do you like honey?

CHUCK: Do I? Boy, I love it.

STR: Well, now I'll have these bees that you see . . .

CHUCK: Bees that I see?

STR: Sure, can't you see them?

CHUCK: Do you?

STR: Certainly. Don't you?

CHUCK: I don't see them, but I know they are there.

STR: How do you know that they are there?

CHUCK: I can hear them walking.

STR: Well, as I said, Chuckie, I'm going to have them give you some honey.

CHUCK: How?

STR: You stand right there, and I'll call the bees in . . .

CHUCK: And they'll sting me.

STR: No, they don't sting you. Now I'll call them in and they'll buzz round you three times. And when they stop, you say give it to me. And you'll get it.

CHUCK: That's all I say. Give it to me, and I'll get it.

STR: That's all. Now, I'll call in the bees (*calls off*), come pretty honey bees, come pretty honey bees.

GIRLS: (*Enter. Each have mouth full of water. Run round Chuck 3 times. Stop.*)

CHUCK: (*Bus.*) When do I get it?

STR: Right now.

CHUCK: (*Bus.*) Alright give it to me.

GIRLS: (*Squirt water in Chuck's face and exit.*)

CHUCK: That's a hell of a joke. (*Wipes water.*)

STR: Oh, oh, Chuck. Look who's coming. Try it on him. (*Exits R.*)

ZEB: (*Enters L.*) Hello Chuckie.

CHUCK: Zebby, old boy. Say, Zeb, do you like honey?

ZEB: Chuck, I love it.

CHUCK: Ha-ha he loves it. Do you want some?

ZEB: Sure, I do.

CHUCK: Alright, stand there and I'll drown you.

ZEB: What's that?

CHUCK: Now, look Zeb see that little room over there? Well, that's where the little bees are. Now I'll buzz round you three times and say humph, then you say give it to me. And you get it.

ZEB: Will I get lots of honey.

CHUCK: Brother, you'll get a hell of a lot more than I got.

ZEB: Oh, alright.

CHUCK: (*Points off R. S.*) Now I'll go over there and get some honey. (*Exits.*)

ZEB: Oh, am I glad I came. I love honey.

CHUCK: (*Enters R. Runs round Zeb three times. Stops each time round and says Humph. Third time spits out water and says.*) You've got to say give it to me.

ZEB: Oh, give it to me.

CHUCK: That's right. Give it to me. (*Exits R.*)

ZEB: Give it to me. Give it to me.

CHUCK: (*Enters, trips, spits out water. Looks at Zeb.*) I slitched. (*Gets another mouth full of water.*)

ZEB: (*Takes out bottle. Gets mouth full of water.*)

CHUCK: (*Enters same bus. After third time round spits out water sore.*) Why the hell don't you say. Give it to me.

ZEB: (*Let's Chuck have it.*)

(*Blackout.*)

NIAGARA FALLS SCENE

CAST: Straight. Juvenile. Comic.
PROPS: Funnel with cork in end. Coin. Pitcher water. Hot water bottle.
OPENING: Straight and juvenile meet C. stage. Shake hands.

Str: Well well: Look who's here. How are you Bill?

Juv: Fine, Jack, and how are you these days?

Str: Just fine Bill. You know Bill, I just joined the finest CLUB. Boy are they a great bunch of fellows.

Juv: Why what CLUB is that Jack?

Str: It's called "THE GRAND AND GLORIOUS CLUB."

Juv: Say, Jack, that sure sounds like a pretty fine CLUB.

Str: Oh, it is Bill. Say, how would you like to join up?

Juv: Oh, I'd love to Jack. What do I have to do?

Str: Well, Bill, I might be able to help you out a whole lot by giving you a little rehearsal first.

Juv: Say, Jack, I would sure appreciate that. Will you?

Str: Why, Bill, it will be a pleasure. Now here. You take this coin, place it on your forehead, bend your head back, and don't straighten your head up until I finish the count of three. Understand?

Juv: Oh, yes, Jack, perfectly.

Str: Okay, Bill, here we go. Bend your head back and place the coin on your head.

Juv: (*Bends head back. Places coin on forehead.*)

Str: (*Places funnel in juvenile's trousers.*) Okay, now, Bill, are you ready?

Juv: READY.

Str: Now, remember, Bill, don't drop the coin until I finish counting THREE.

Juv: Okay, Jack, I know.

Str: Alright here we go. ONE . . . TWO. (*Pours water in funnel.*) Wet leg bus.

Juv: Ah, that's a dirty trick, Jack. (*Runs off stage. Comes back with funnel in his hand.*) Say, Jack, does (COMIC) know this one?

Str: No. I'm sure he doesn't.

Juv: Oh, Oh, Jack, here he comes now. Let's try it on him. (*Comic enters. Goes through same talk and business as before. Puts funnel in top of hot water bag which is hidden in Comic's trousers.*) Now are you ready?

Com: READY.

Juv: Okay, here we go. One . . . (*Pours water. Comic doesn't move.*) Two . . . (*Pours water again. Comic doesn't move.*) Juvenile and straight work this up big.) Three. . . (*Pours water. Comic straightens up head. Drops coin in funnel out of trousers. Laughs at Straight and Juvenile.*)

Com: Huh: I heard that one before. (*They all exit.*)

(*Blackout.*)

---

3 x 3 ARE TEN

Str. enters from one side of stage with three hats. 1st comic enters from opposite side. They meet C.

Str: Say: Where is there a good hatter at around here?

Com: A good whater?

Str: A hatter. Don't you understand? I want to find some place to take these ten hats to get cleaned.

Com: How many hats did you say?

Str: Ten.

Com: Huh: I only see three.

Str: Well, of course, in reality there are only three, but you know three times three are ten?

Com: Three times three is how much?

Str: Ten, I said.

Com: Boy: where did you go to school? If ever?

Str: Why, I went thru grammar school. High school. And I spent one year in college.

Com: And still you mean to stand there with your bare face hanging out, and say that three times three are ten?

Str: That's just exactly what I said.

Com: It won't be long now.

Str: Well, I'll just bet you ten dollars that three times three are ten.

Com: It's a shame to take the money. But I'm a sport.

Str: (*Takes out money.*) There's my ten.

Com: (*Takes out money.*) Oh, make it ten more. (*Money betting gag.*) Now I'll bet you that and raise you ten. (*Picks up bill.*)

Str: (*Stops him.*) Come on. M.O.F.

Com: Huh?

Str: I said M.O.F.

Com: What's that M.O.F. business?

Str: Money on the floor.

Com: (*Puts money back on floor.*)

Str: Alright, now watch. (*Lays down hats. One at a time. Starting from the R. 1—2—3, then start from R. again and count 4. But let that hat stay on the floor. Then on the next two. 5—6. Pick them up and hold them. Then back to the one on the floor and pick it up on 7. Lay it down on 8. Then lay the other two down that you have in your hand on 9. 10. Pick up money and laugh at Comic.*) Well, thanks old man, I sure need this.

Com: Wait a minute. (*Counts the same as Str. did.*) Yep: your right.

Str: (*Laughs and exits counting money.*)

2nd: (*Enters.*) Say: Where are you going with those three hats?

Com: How many did you say you see?

2nd: Why three.

Com: You're crazy. There's ten hats here.

2nd: How do you figure that out?

Com: Well, I know there's only three but ain't three times three ten?

2nd: Not so you could notice it.

Com: (*Aside.*) Oh, Oh, Easy Money. I'll bet you $10.00 that 3x3 are 10.

2nd: And I'll just bet you ten dollars, three times three are not ten.

Com: (*Starts counting and gets it all balled up. Counts like this. Has all three hats in hand. Starts to lay down from R. and count 1—2—3—goes back to the R. again. 4—5—leaves those two lay. Picks up 6. Back to the R. again and picks up 7—8—. You now have all three in hand. From the R. lay down 9—10—Eleven. Holds it for laugh.*)

2nd: (*Picks up money and laughs.*) Well, I'll be seeing you later. Thanks for the spending money. (*Exits.*)

Com: (*Pays no attention to 2nd. Comic looks at hats. Scratches head. Finally does it over again. Each time he gets more numbers. Finally says.*) Ah, hell. (*Exits. Black out.*)

IZZY-WUZZY SCENE

CAST: Comic. Straight.
OPENING: Comic and Straight enter meet center stage.

Str: Well, Hello, Hello. Oh, by the way I forgot your name. Oh, no, I didn't.
What is your name? Now, don't tell me. Don't tell me. (*Bus. Thinking.*)
Com: Huh: he don't know my name is ABIE COHN.
Str: That's right: ABIE COHN. And you're from? Let's see. Now don't tell
me. (*Same bus. of thinking.*)
Com: Can you imagine? He don't know I'M from NEW YORK.
Str: That's right: Little ABIE COHN from NEW YORK. By the way, ABIE,
how is your sister?
Com: Which one? Becky . . . Agnes . . . or Mabel?
Str: Why, BECKY. How is she?
Com: Oh, she's fine: she's married and got TWINS.
Str: You don't tell me.
Com: But I did tell you.
Str: How old are the TWINS?
Com: One is SIX. And one is FOUR.
Str: What are their names?
Com: IZZY and WUZZY.
Str: IZZY and WUZZY. Well, how are they?
Com: Well last week IZZY was sick. But he's alright now. But when I left the
house this morning, WUZZY was sick.
Str: Oh, Izzy?
Com: No, Wuzzy.
Str: That's what I said: Is he?
Com: No, Wuzzy. Izzy was sick last week.
Str: Oh: was he?
Com: No, Izzy.
Str: I thought you said, Wuzzy was sick.
Com: Wuzzy was sick. But now Izzy is sick.
Str: Oh, Wuzzy was sick? Izzy?
Com: (*Works this up big with Straight.*) Oh, they're both dead.
(*They exit. Comic very disgusted.*)

(*Blackout.*)

PRICKLY HEAT

CAST: Chuck, Str., Juv., Ing.
SET: In two. Office desk. Chair back desk. Phone. 2 chairs. Juv. has foot
wrapped up. Str. has head wrapped round. As curtain goes up, phone rings.

Ing: (*Answers phone.*) Hello: Yes, this is Dr. Cuttem's office. No, Dr. Cuttem
 is out of town, but his assistant is here.
Str: Oh, that's the guy that ruined me.
Juv: Yes, and he sure ruined me too. Say what did he do to you?
Str: Oh, I came in here and told him I had erisiplas, and he cut my ear off.
 (*Bus.*) Say, what did he do to you?
Juv: He did the same thing to me. I came in here and told him I had ptomane
 poisoning and he cut my toe off. (*Both cry bus.*)
Ing: (*Bell offstage.*) Come in.
Chuck: (*Enters bus. X's to nurse.*) Is the doctor in?
Ing: No: But his assistant is in.
Str: (*And Juv.*) Oh, that assistant. (*Bus.*) Look out for that assistant.
Chuck: Why, what's the matter mister?
Str: (*Str. explains again about his ear.*)
Chuck: (*To Juv.*) And what happened to you?
Juv: (*Explains about his toe.*)
Chuck: (*Repeats both cases. Turns to nurse.*) So long Letty. (*Starts to ex.*)
Ing: (*Grabs Chuck.*) Why, what's the matter?
Chuck: Lady, there's nothing wrong with me, in fact I never felt better in my
 life.
Ing: I know. But there must have been something wrong with you when you
 came in.
Chuck: Weel, Lady, I didn't feel so good when I first came in. But I'm alright
 now.
Ing: Well, come with me.
Chuck: Oh, well that's different.
Ing: Now what's wrong?
Chuck: (*Goes over the two men again.*)
Ing: That's right.
Chuck: Lady, that doctor can't do me a damn bit of good.
Ing: Why not?
Chuck: I got prickly heat.

(*Blackout.*)

THE PHOTOGRAPH GALLERY
Bob Noell's Version

CAST: Straight, Jake

PROPERTIES: Bogus camera; black cloth to use with camera; two-sided "photograph" with sketch of Jake on one side and a donkey's head on the other; a table; a chair.

STRAIGHT: I've rigged up a bogus camera and as soon as I can rope someone in, I'll raise enough money to get out of this town. Here comes someone now. (*Stands erect and looks important as Jake enters.*)

JAKE: I brung 'em.

STRAIGHT: You brought *what*?

JAKE: 'Taters.

STRAIGHT: You brought potatoes?

JAKE: Yep. I put 'em in the cellar.

STRAIGHT: I didn't order any potatoes!

JAKE: Yes, you DID!

STRAIGHT: That's a laugh! Whatever made you think I ordered potatoes?

JAKE: I seen it on the sign out there: "POTATOES TAKEN HERE."

STRAIGHT: (*Laughs.*) Oh! hahaha, Jake, that doesn't say "potatoes." That sign says "Photographs Taken Here."

JAKE: Oh, I ain't got none of them!

STRAIGHT: No, you don't understand! This is a photograph gallery! Tell you what I'll do! I'll take your picture.

JAKE: No, you don't. You don't get no picture of mine. I done told you I ain't got none!

STRAIGHT: Jake, how much are the potatoes in the cellar?

JAKE: Three dollars! Pay me or I'll leave!

STRAIGHT: Now, Jake. Wouldn't you like to have a nice picture of yourself to give to your girl?

JAKE: Ha ha! Dat would be nice, wouldn't it? But where I gonna get one?

STRAIGHT: Right here. That's what I do. See that black box over there?

JAKE: Yeah, I see it all right. What is it?

STRAIGHT: That's the camera.

(*Jake sidles cautiously around the Straight, putting the Straight between himself and the camera and then peeks at the camera. Business.*)

STRAIGHT: What's the matter Jake?

JAKE: I ain't never monkeyed around with no cannon before.

STRAIGHT: Oh Jake, don't be silly. Now, I can make a picture that will look *just like you!*

JAKE: You can? How much do dey cost?

STRAIGHT: Well, the first dozen is ten dollars; the second dozen is five dollars; and the third dozen is free.

JAKE: I'll take some of the third dozen first.

STRAIGHT: No, Jake. But I'll tell you what I *will* do; I'll make you *one* picture for the potatoes in the cellar!

JAKE: Will it look like me?

STRAIGHT: I promise.

JAKE: (*Business.*) Haha, gonna give it to my gal!

STRAIGHT: OK, Jake, please sit in front of the camera.

(*Jake starts to exit.*)

STRAIGHT: Wait a minute, Jake, where are you going?

JAKE: I dunno, but I ain't sittin' in front of no *cannon*.

STRAIGHT: JAKE! This is the box that makes the picture, not a *cannon*. It's a camera. Now please take a chair.

JAKE: Don't mind if I do. (*Picks up chair and starts to exit while the Straight has his head under the black cloth.*)

STRAIGHT: (*Coming out from under the cloth.*) Here! Here! What are you doing?

JAKE: You said take a seat.

STRAIGHT: No, I meant "take a chair and sit down."

(*Jake sits on floor with chair in lap, muttering happily, "gonna give it to my gal!" Straight comes out from under cloth several times, each time in a bewildered search for his hyperactive "subject." Finally the Straight finds him.*)

STRAIGHT: JAKE! What are you doing on the floor?

JAKE: (*Angrily.*) You *said* to take a chair and sit down! I'se done what you SAID!

STRAIGHT: No! No! No! (*Exasperated.*) I mean, "SIT ON THE CHAIR!"

JAKE: Why the devil didn't you say so in the first place! (*To audience.*) Gonna give it to my gal, ha ha.

(*Straight is under the black cloth again, "focusing" on Jake. Waves hand over camera to Jake. Jake laughs and says, "Dat's nice, she's waving at me." Gets up, shakes hands with the Straight. Straight untangles self from cloth and angrily shouts, "What on earth do you think you're doing?"*)

JAKE: You was waving yer hand at me.

STRAIGHT: (*Trying to contain temper, softens voice menacingly and says.*) Jake, when I wave my hand this way (*palm down*), it means LOWER, LOWER, LOWER. When I wave my hand *this* way (*palm up*), it means HIGHER, HIGHER, HIGHER. And so forth and so on. (*Waves hand side to side.*)

JAKE: Hope there ain't too much "so forth and so on."

(*Straight, under the cloth again, waves his hand "higher, higher, higher." Jake raises himself a little each time the hand is waved, and finally ends up sitting perched on the chair back with his feet on the seat, still chuckling, "Gonna give it to my gal, haha." Straight untangles again.*)

STRAIGHT: (*Angrily.*) Jake, we're never going to get this picture made if you don't stop your foolishness. What are you doing NOW?

JAKE: You SAID "Higher," and this is the highest I could get.

STRAIGHT: Please, Jake, SIT DOWN.

(*Jake mumbles "gonna give it to my gal" to the audience as he sits. The Straight waves his hand "lower, lower, lower." Jake keeps moving down until he is lying flat on the floor.*)

JAKE: Doggone it, quit waving—I can't *git* no lower!

STRAIGHT: (*Untangles. Almost cries.*) Jake, I'm going to try *it one more time.* Please—*You* sit still and *I'll move the camera.*

(*Jake grins at the audience: "haha, gonna give it to my gal." Straight gets under the cloth again. He moves the box up and down trying to "find" his subject. Meanwhile, Jake jumps up, yelling.*)

JAKE: HOT DOG! I found another one!

STRAIGHT: (Untangles.) Another what?

JAKE: I found another pin with the point pointing toward me! That's good luck! My Ma says if I find a thousand pins with the point pointing toward me I'll get a brand-new automobile. I done found nine hundred and ninety-eight pins! All I need is two more!

STRAIGHT: (*Stares at Jake for a moment and shakes head.*) Well, OK. Now are we ready to try again?

JAKE: Oh, yeah. De picture. Yeah—just need *two more pins!* Ain't dat sumpin? (*Straight goes under. More business with camera. Jake jumps up, excited.*) Doggone! Dere's another pin with the point right toward me! (*Straight untangles, sneaks behind Jake. Business of taking pin out from under collar and fixing it in chair so Jake will "get the point." All the while Jake is in ecstacy over his luck, mumbling, "All I need is ONE MORE PIN." Lots of funny business here of Straight watching in anticipation as Jake starts to sit, then gets up. Several tense moments. Each time Jake rises he asks the Straight a new question: "Will it look like me?" "Will my gal like it?" "I ain't gonna pay if it don't look like me!" "You sure she'll like it?" "Can I get it right away or do I hafta wait?" Finally, when he sits, Jake bounces straight up with a yowl.*)

STRAIGHT: (*Snickering.*) What's the matter, Jake?

JAKE: I found the other pin. (*Pause for laughter.*) With the point right toward me.

STRAIGHT: OK, now let's get back to the picture.

(*Jake, rubbing the seat of his pants, turns and runs his hand all over the chair seat, then slides across the seat and says "ahh." Turns to audience, smiles, and says, "Gonna give it to my gal, haha!" Straight goes under cloth, then moves the camera. Jake peers into it inquisitively. Straight untangles.*)

STRAIGHT: Jake, you were looking right into the camera. That's bad. Let's see. Oh, yes—do you see that fly on the wall behind the camera?

JAKE: (*Cranes his neck.*) No, I don't see him, but I know he's there.

STRAIGHT: If you can't see him, *how* do you know he's there?

JAKE: I can hear him walking.

STRAIGHT: Jake! I know you can see that fly. NOW, KEEP YOUR EYE ON THAT FLY. (*Straight goes under the cloth just as Jake's fly takes flight. Jake stands and moves his head rapidly, watching the fly's erratic flight, then, as the Straight untangles and watches, faces the audience and says, "Cain't be done! Cain't be done!"*)

STRAIGHT: *What* can't be done?

JAKE: Cain't keep my eye on the fly.

STRAIGHT: Why not?

JAKE: (*Pointing to a child in the audience.*) That little boy down there swallowed it.

STRAIGHT: Jake, enough of this nonsense! See the knothole on the wall?

JAKE: Yep.

STRAIGHT: OK, keep your eye on that knothole. (*Goes under.*)

JAKE: Doggone! Always did like to peep through knotholes—see a lot of funny things that way. (*He walks over to the wall and puts his eye to the knothole. Straight untangles and asks Jake what he is doing. Jake argues.*)

STRAIGHT: Jake, just sit still. (*Goes under. He slaps the table loudly under the camera and pulls out the hand-sketched portrait of Jake.*)

JAKE: (*Angrily.*) Dat don't look like me!

STRAIGHT: I say it does!

JAKE: DON'T!

STRAIGHT: DOES!

JAKE: DON'T! Etc.

(*Finally the Straight appeals to the front row, which was always made up of children.*)

STRAIGHT: Doesn't this look like Jake?

JAKE: No!

CHILDREN: Yes!

JAKE: No!

CHILDREN: Yes!

JAKE: (*Finally, to Straight.*) All right den, if DAT (*indicating the picture*) looks like ME, den DIS (*flipping the picture to reveal the donkey head on the back*) looks like YOU.

THE BULL FIGHT

(*Straight enters L., Comic R.*)

Str: AH, COHEN, I see you are in Mexico again. What are you doing here?

Com: Came here to look over the black eyed Senoritas.

Str: Is that all you came for?

Com: It's none of your business.

Str: You know today is the day of the big bull fight.

Com: Oh, here's where they throw the bull.

Str: Yes, they throw the bull—No, they don't throw the bull here.

Com: Oh, they shoot the bull.

Str: Yes, they shoot the bull—no, they don't shoot the bull. You see today all the bull fighters went on strike.

Com: Oh, then you're out of a job.

Str: Yes, I'm out of a job—No, I told you I didn't shoot the bull. Now that all the bull fighters are on a strike, today you're going to fight the bull.

Com: No, I'm not going to fight no bull.

Str: You'll fight the bull or I'll fill you full of holes. (*Bus. with gun.*) Which?

Com: I'll fight the bull.

Str: Good.

Com: No, bad. But you should never kill a bull.

Str: Why?

Com: Because it makes widows out of cows.

Str: I'll teach you the art of fighting the bulls. Now the arena is crowded with people. Thousands upon thousands. All the people are sitting in tiers.

Com: The tears were rolling down their backs.

Str: Hell no. How can tears roll down their backs?

Com: They were all cock eyed.

Str: First there's a large blast of trumpets. Out come the Matidors.

Com: Out come the Matidors.

Str: Then there's another blast of trumpets and out come the Picidors.

Com: And out come the Picidors.

Str: Then there's another large blast of trumpets and out come the—

Com: Cuspadors.

Str: Out come the Cuspadors—Hell, no, there's no Cuspadors in this.

Com: Well, don't the bull chew?

Str: Certainly the bull chews.

Com: Well, the bull's got to spit.

Str: The bull doesn't spit. Then there's another large blast of trumpets and out comes the bull.

Com: Then you come out.

Str: Then I come out—No, I don't come out. Now the fight is on. The bull charges at the Matidor, the Matidor pulls out his Machuka.

Com: He does what?

Str: He pulls out his Machuka.

Com: The Dirty thing, and there are women there.

Str: Certainly there are women there. Now you'll have to have one.

Com: Oh, I've got one.

Str: Is it a good one?

Com: You Damn Right.

Str: Is It A Long One?

Com: Oh, It's About That . . . (*Bus.*) What the hell do you want to know for?

Str: Well, you see I must examine your Machuka before you go in the Arena.

Com: I don't know you well enough.

Str: Come on, just lay it in my hand. I won't drop it.

Com: But if you do, don't drop it in the mud.

Str: Well, I must see it. Where is your Machuka?

Com: I left it at home.

Str: You left it home? Well then, in that case you'll have to use my Machuka.

Com: Your Machuka? Hell no, I wouldn't touch it. Where's your Machuka?

Str: Here it is. (*Bus. of handing him sabre.*)

Com: Oh, is that your Machuka?

Str: Certainly, what did you think I meant?

Com: Same thing.

Str: Now the bull charges the Matidor, the Matidor sticks the bull in the eye.

Com: Oh, it's a bull's eye.

Str: Yes, it's—no, it's not a bull's eye. Then the bull becomes more enraged and charges the Matidor once again. This time the Matidor stabs the bull in the back of the neck with his Bandrillo.

Com: Oh, he sticks the bull in the back with his umbrella.

Str: Yes, with his—no, not his umbrella, with his Bandrillo. Then the bull rushes over here, (*bus. from L. to R.*) then the bull rushes over here. (*Bus. to R.*) Then the bull rushes over here. (*Bus. of throwing Comic L.*)

Com: Oh, he's in the bull rushes.

Str: That's it, in the bull rushes.

Com: And where was Moses?

Str: There was no Moses. Moses was a Biblical character, Pharro's daughter found Moses in the bull rushes.

Com: That's what she said—and she got away with it.

Str: Here's your sword. (*Cheer offstage.*) And here comes the crowd to cheer you on to victory. (*Enter all principals R.*) Now folks, I want to make you acquainted with (*Comic*) who is going to fight the bull today. (*Cheer from crowd. Three hurrahs.*)

Com: You can keep your hurrahs to yourself, I don't fight the bull. (*Disgusted bahs from crowd.*) I'd rather have them say there he goes than doesn't he look natural.

2nd Com: (*Rushes in.*) Comic. Comic. I just told all the bulls that you were going to fight them and they all dropped dead. (*Exits.*)

Com: Folks, I'm going to fight the bulls. (*Hurrahs from crowd.*) Bring on your bulls, bulls with big horns, the bigger they come the better I like 'em. Bulls that weigh two thousand pounds, Bulls with big Machukas, what the hell do I care? (*Hurrahs from crowd.*)

2nd Com: (*Rushes on. To Comic.*) No, I made a mistake, the bulls are not dead. They are alive and raring and snorting to go.

Com: Why don't you make up your mind what these bulls are going to do? No folks I don't fight no bulls today.

Str: (*Bus. with gun.*) You'll fight that bull or I'll fight you full of lead. Which?

Com: I'll fight the bull. (*Exit L.*)

Str: (*Over looking off right with rest of cast.*) Look at the way that boy goes in to the arena, look they are letting the bull in to the arena, (*Comic*) why just see how he jumped right over the bull's back, the bull's charging at (*Comic*). Look. He pulled out his Bandrillo and is shaking it in the bull's face. Now look he stuck the bull in the rear with his Machuka. The bull is bleeding, the bull is down, he's up, he's down, he's down (etc.). The bull is dead.

Hurrah for (*Comic.*).

Com: (*Enters L. with coat off.*) How the hell do you find the gate?

(*Blackout.*)

THE SKETCH

Further elaboration of a bit—or an assemblage of several bits—resulted in the sketch, which extended and complicated the device of a joke developed by a Comic and a Straight. In the sketch the comedy duo plus a number of auxiliary characters were sometimes involved in a loosely-knit story with at least some pretensions to credibility and plot development—in effect a one-act play. But such refinements were often no more critical issues than in the bit. Consider, for example, the popular court room and school room sketches seen so often in many types of popular entertainment. Although some of them ran as long as half an hour or more and involved ten or a dozen performers, they were essentially nothing more than "anthologies" of bits, all fitted together within the framing device of a trial or a grammar school class. Even those which had a nodding acquaintance with actual plot and characterization were generally so fluid as to make the addition or subtraction of material quite easy.

The "school act" or "kid scene" was made famous early in the twentieth century by the Avon Comedy Four, a group that numbered among its members the legendary Smith and Dale. Chuck Callahan's "School Days" sketch, which is very much in the tradition of the Avon Comedy Four routines, is basically nothing more than an open-ended collection of comedy material and song, tied together by a slim classroom theme. In many ways it is not much more complex than the schoolroom sequence that forms a part of the Madden's act in the previous section. In the Callahan sketch, however, eight characters are involved rather than two, a simple setting is called for, and there is a kind of rock-bottom consistency about roles and about an illusion of reality which is not present in the Madden routine. Here we are *in* a school room, not simply listening to a performer repeat what he did there.

"The Black Breach of Promise Case" is a more elaborate version of the same "revue" idea, this time focused around the device of a trial. The mock trial was a hallowed institution in many forms of popular entertainment, often done with an Irish cast or in blackface. Versions of the basic trial routine not too different from this one were performed in recent memory on television by the late "Pigmeat" Markham, and on Broadway in Ralph Allen's burlesque musical *Sugar Babies*.

The remainder of the sketches in this section are more clearly related to the one-act play tradition—given, of course, that there was always ample room for the introduction of songs, gags, bits and the like. The famous "Three O'Clock Train" is one of the best-loved sketches from the popular tradition. There are countless variations of this ancient ghost routine, in both blackface and whiteface. Every comic felt free to use it as a vehicle for his own favorite bits of business, and in fact, it usually ran much longer than the version printed here might suggest.

I once saw the late comic "Greasy" Medlin perform a version of the "Three O'Clock Train" sketch in which the climax was an extraordinary bit of his own. In the bit Greasy showed the Straight how he went about courting his girl. He threw himself into the spirit of the occasion, demonstrating to the Straight precisely how he put his arm around the girl and how he went about giving her a kiss. In the meantime the Straight had slipped away and Greasy wound up making passionate love to the ghost. It was a moment of outrageous physical comedy worthy of the *commedia dell'arte*. In fact, many sketches centered around similar pieces of elaborate physical comedy. In another ghost sketch, "Pete in the Well," for example, the Comic and Straight are involved in a complicated, almost balletic pantomime bit; and "Over the "River, Charlie" contains a mock operation of *commedia*-like complexity. In a burlesque sketch, "Cluck's Sanitarium Scene," the time-honored operation theme is expanded and a certain amount of mild sexual innuendo is introduced, as befitted a sketch aimed at a predominantly male audience.

"Dot Quied Lotgings" was published by a firm that specialized in providing material for "parlor theatricals"—the amateur market. But the piece is typical of the sketches that were played as afterpieces in early vaudeville, in medicine shows, and in other variety entertainments. It contains typical "Dutch," Irish and English stereotypes. The last item in this section, a classic burlesque of *Uncle Tom's Cabin*, is the kind of sketch that was often used as a minstrel show afterpiece. The sketch involves not only parody of the famous old play, but also of minstrelsy and of the stock Irish comedy character. The piece is a type known in the late nineteenth century as "slam-bang, knock-down farce," with the emphasis on low comedy, bizarre characters and outrageous situations.

SCHOOL DAYS

CAST: Straight. Juvenile. Ingenue. Comic. Four Girls.
PROPS: Eight desks. Blackboard. Books. Apple.
OPENING: All singing schooldays. Teacher enters after opening song.

Teacher: (*Enters.*) Good morning scholars.

All: Good morning, Teacher.

Teacher: We will now have our singing exercise. (*Do number here. After number.*) But where is Chuck?

Chuck: (*Enters.*) Good morning, Teacher.

Teacher: Chuckie, why are you late?

Chuck: My mother lost the lid to the stove and I had to sit on the hole to keep the smoke from coming out. You know, Teacher, I get blamed for everything that happens down at our house. The other day my sister fell down and hurt her knee. I got blamed for that. Yesterday, my brother cut his finger. I got blamed for it. This morning the cat had kittens, I . . . (*laughs this up*) had to drown them. And you know, Teacher, they are always fighting down at my house. Every night when my father comes home from work he fights with my mother. The other night my father came home, started a fight and hit my mother so hard he knocked her unconscious.

Teacher: Chuck, who is your father?

Chuck: That's what they're always fighting about.

Teacher: Well, now we will have our spelling lesson. (*Chuck takes punch on gag, feet on desk bus.*) Chuckie take your feet off the desk. (*Chuck pays no attention.*) Chuckie take your feet off that desk.

Chuck: Oh, it's my desk, isn't it?

Teacher: Yes.

Chuck: Well, what do you want?

Teacher: I want you to take your feet off that desk.

Chuck: Now, let me tell you something Teach. You know my Dad pays taxes to keep this school running. And the people pay you your salary. I am the people. You'll admit that you are a public servant?

Teacher: Yes, I am a public servant.

Chuck: Well, get me a glass of water.

Teacher: Chuckie, you are a very bad boy. And just for being naughty, I want you to stay after school. And, what you'll get is nobody's business.

Chuck: Well, nobody has to know what happens.

Teacher: Oh, I wish I was your mother for fifteen minutes.

Chuck: Okay, Teach, I'll speak to my dad and see if I can fix it.

Teacher: Now, girls, report to Mrs. Walters for your cooking lessons. (*Girls exit.*) Chuckie, I want you to come up to the blackboard and write the word strictly. And if you write it correctly after school I will give you a nice big dish of ice cream.

Chuck: You want me to write the word stritly?

Teacher: No, Chuckie. It's strictly. Now, if you write it correctly when I come back from the principal's office, you will get your ice cream. (*Exits.*)

Chuck: (*Runs up to the blackboard.*) Oh boy, I'm goin' to get ice cream. (*Picks up *chalk.*) S. .T. .R. .I. .C. .T. .L. . Say, Gene, what's the last letter?

Gene: Why.

Chuck: So I can finish the word.

Gene: Well, why.

Chuck: Maybe I forgot it.

Gene: Chuckie, it isn't possible for you to forget it.

Chuck: Why isn't it possible for me to forget it?

Gene: Because I told you. WHY.

Chuck: You told me, WHY?

Gene: That's right.

Chuck: Well, what's the answer?

Gene: That's the answer.

Chuck: Oh, that. (*Goes to board to put it at end of word. Stops.*) Hey, Gene, you can't put that at the end of this. (*Points.*)

Gene: I didn't tell you to put that at the end of there.

Chuck: (*Muggs this.*) Well, you said that, was WHY.

Gene: Yes, but when I say why, I don't mean WHY.

Chuck: (*Muggs this.*) Oh no?

Gene: No; I mean why.

Chuck: (*Muggs this also.*) When you say why you don't mean why? What kind of dizzy people are you? Listen, when I say you're crazy, I don't mean you're crazy.

Gene: No?

Chuck: No. You're nutty. Come on, Gene, tell me the last letter.

Gene: Chuck, are you still in a quandry about that last letter?

Chuck: Yeh: I'm still in a Foundry.

Gene: I don't see how anybody can look so healthy and be so dumb.

Chuck: Well, I take care of myself . . . Say who's dumb? I didn't ask you any questions to be insulted. All I want to know is the last letter. Do you know what it is?

Gene: I do.

Chuck: Well, will you please tell me what it is?

Gene: I will. (*Makes motion as though to start talking.*)

Chuck: Don't ask me now. I ask you answers, and you tell me questions. Come on Gene tell me the last letter.

Gene: Alright, I'll tell you. Now this is the last time. (*Goes over to Chuck.*) Take off your hat. Why is it that men like you and I have tried to find out the whys and wherefores? Why? Why is why. Put on your hat. But up till now we have never been able to find out why why is why. So therefore we come to the conclusion that why is why because it's why and therefore it couldn't be anything else but why. Take off your hat. (*Hat bus. Gene puts hands on Chuck's chest.*) Now on the other hand. (*Chuck changes hat to other hand.*) or rather on the other hand. (*Chuck changes back.*) If you knew why why was why, you wouldn't be standing there asking me, and I wouldn't be standing here trying to tell you. So, therefore, we come to the conclusion that why is why because it's why and therefore it couldn't be anything else but why. Put on your hat. But on the other hand, we . . .

Chuck: (*Gets sore, throws hat down on stage.*) What has the hat got to do with it? What kind of a conversation is this? (*Bus. Chuck puts hands on Gene's chest.*) Why is why because you put on the hat. Why is why because you take off the hat. So, therefore, we come to the conclusion that why is why because it couldn't be you. And it couldn't be I. So, therefore, we come to the conclusion that why is why and the Democratic people are for the people, by the people, and the constitution of the Government and why. (*Chuck puts hands back on Gene's chest*) Look, Gene, what I want to find out is Y . . . Oh, you mean Y. A WE with a tail on it.

Gene: Don't take you long to catch on does it? Certainly, that's what I meant.

Chuck: Well, why didn't you say so in the first place? (*Marks it up, goes back to seat.*)

Teacher: (*Enters. Looks at board.*) Well, now, that's very good Chuckie.

Gene: Teacher, I brought you this nice big Apple. (*Tosses it to her, she drops it, stoops over and picks it up. Back to boys. Gene laughs.*)

Teacher: Gene, what are you laughing at?

Gene: Oh, Teacher, I saw your garter.

Teacher: Gene Morgan, you take your books and go home for two weeks.

Gene: (*Exits saying.*) Oh, Teacher, I don't want to go home.

Teacher: (*Same stooping bus. Juv. laughs.*) Now, what are you laughing at young man?

Juv: Oh, Teacher, I saw your leg above your garter.

Teacher: Well, you take your hat and books and go home for three months. (*Juv. same exit. Teacher sits up on high stool. She crosses legs. Chuck picks up hat, starts.*) Chuckie, where are you going?

Chuck: Teacher, my schooldays are over forever.

(*Blackout.*)

THE BLACK
BREACH OF PROMISE CASE
A Negro Farce

CHARACTERS:
Judge
Clerk of Court
Attorney Snowball
Attorney Brass
Josephus Jellybrain, Plaintiff

Peter Periwinkle
Crier
Policeman
Jury
Seraphina Sugarplum, Defendant

PLAYS TWENTY-FIVE MINUTES

Judge on the bench, underneath him the Clerk, Jury on R., beneath whom are seats for Counsel, Plaintiff, Defendant, etc. Witness Box on L., with Policeman in attendance. Crier. Books and papers scattered about tables. Large inkstand, for judge, made of pasteboard.

Judge: Am de jury all dissembled?
Police: Dey am, yer washup.
Judge: Did ye swear dem all?
Police: Yes, dey's all bin swearin' for de last half-hour, some ob dem berry badly.
Judge: Call de case.
Clerk: Jellybrain *versus* Sugarplum.
Crier: Silence! Jellybrain an' Sugarplum, come into court!
(*Enter Attorneys Snowball and Brass, followed by Josephus Jellybrain and Seraphina Sugarplum, who take seats.*)
Judge: What am dis about? (*Takes up pen, dips it into a large inkstand, and after jabbing the point on the desk two or three times, pretends to write.*)
Clerk: Dis am a case ob breach ob promise ob marriage, yer honor, the plaintiff bein' Josephus Jellybrain an' de defendant Seraphina Sugarplum.
Snowball: I appears for the plaintiff, your honor!
Judge: Does yer? Den dat am a bad job for *him*.
Jelly: (*Jumps up.*) Eh, what de—
Crier: Silence! (*Jellybrain collapses.*)
Brass: I am for de defendant, your honor.
Judge: I doesn't happen to be in possession ob yer name.
Brass: Brass, your honor.
Judge: (*Writes.*) I might hab guessed it by yer face — why, I declare I've left out de fust two letters an' put it down "ass," but it won't matter. Brudder Snowball, you'd better open your case.
Snow: (*Rising.*) Your honor, and gentlemen ob de jury—Dis am one ob de most 'scruciatin' cases dat eber I remember in all my long susperience ob de outraged laws ob cibilised sassiety—dat ob a lubin', trustin' an' manly buzum bein' converted into a skaotic mass of trubble by de act ob a shemale, who, aldough wearin' de form ob a human bein'—
Brass: I takes objection to de term "human bein'," my lud, my client am a lady.

Snow: Den, your honor, an' gentlemen ob de jury, dis lady who am *not* a human bein', hab so played upon de feelins ob my client, Josephus Jellybrain, dat de place where his heart once existed am now a complete vackyum, full ob nuffin but grief an' despair. He may beat his manly buzzum from mornin' till night, but he can't get no relief—

Juryman: Why can't he go to the doctor, den?

Snow: For what-relief? Can a doctor-relief heal a broken heart? No—he can't eben pick up de bits! Can he renew blighted hopes? No—he can't sake blight off a potator! Can he bring back joys dat am for eber flown? No—he couldn't eben clip dero wings! My client had delicate feelins; he was a poet, but de divine inflatus am now departed, driven from its temples by de rude hands of Seraphina Sugarplum.

Judge: How thankful he ought ter be!

Snow: He was surprised, you honor, by de bref ob nature's sweetest music—in his buzzum dwelt de spirit ob Parnassus.

Brass: An' plenty more.

Snow: Plenty more what?

Brass: Asses.

Snow: You's a calumny hater, brudder Brass. We shall show, by de clearest ebidence, dat my client, Josephus Jellybrain, was a poet ob de finest mold.

Brass: Yes, his poetry was berry mouldy.

Judge: Dese interruptions am berry unseemly.

Snow: We shall show dat de first meeting between my client and de unprincipled shemale defendant, who has wrecked his happiness and ruined his appetite, was caricatured by lub at first sight, when, struck by the extinguished appearance ob de defendant at a ball, he gabe vent to his feelins in the follerin' beautiful couplet, which he placed in her hand, written on a caramel wrapper—

"De moon am shinin' bright,
Can I see yer home to-night?"

If dis, your honor, isn't a proof ob lub at fust sight, I should like to know what am? Den what did she reply? I'd like yer, gentlemen ob de jury, to pay 'ticklar attention to it. Catchin' de divine inflatus from my 'complished client, she quickly returned de sugared missive, wif the addition—

"De stars am shinin' too,
So I don't mind if yer do."

Now, your honor, can any sane pusson doubt de significance ob der exchange ob sentiments? Here am a distinct engagement in writing, entered into by bofe parties, deliberately, an' wivout malice aforethought! De eyyes ob de defendant had kindled in my client's breast dose flames which nuffin can distinguish an' against which dere am no insurance; for a little later we finds him penning de follerin' beautiful confusion—

"In a deep vale, shut out by old pine treeses,
Near a big pond, whar floats de ducks an' geeses,

Whar hickory nuts an' sweet potaters grows,
An' de essence ob de sunflower greets de nose;
In our log hut we'd pass de happy hours,
An murmur what a jolly life was ours;
We'd breave our lub unto de stars an' moon,
An' eat our supper off a roasted coon.''

But perversity, gentlemen ob de jury, dwells in all shemale buzzoms! Josephus Jellybrain's dream ob hot cakes, warm beds, comfortable slippers, smokin' coffee, well-buttoned shirts, redeemed stockins, bootjacks an' happiness faded into de past, into a future ob cold sheets, frozen bones, heelless socks, gutta percha biscuits, tough steaks, corns, coughs, rhubard, aloes, an' misery! De pictur am too appallin' ter dwell upon, an' I'll not harrow yer minds by doin' so; but dis wreck ob all human hopes hab been brought about by Seraphina Sugarplum. Gentlemen, yer might as well try to ladle a riber dry wiv a teaspoon, to twist yer heel inter de toe ob yer boot, remember whar yer's left yer umbrella when it's rainin', or anyfing else dat's considered impossible, as to coax a woman to do somefing when she says she won't. Your honor, I shall now place my client in de witness box.—Call Josephus Jellybrain.

Crier: Josephus Jellybag!

Police: Peter Jellyfish!

Jelly: (*Goes into witness box.*) I's here, what's left of me. (*During the whole of the evidence the Judge now and then dips his pen in the inkstand, jabs the point on the desk, and pretends to write.*)

Snow: Your name is Josephus Jellybrain?

Jelly: I allers thought so.

Judge: No lebbity, sir; answer de squestion, yes or no?

Jelly: Yes—or no.

Judge: What do yer mean by dat?

Jelly: I's tryin' to answer as you want me to do.

Judge: Am you the plaintiff in dis action?

Jelly: Yes, sar. It am a berry *plain tiff* between me an' de lady, sure enuff.

Snow: How long hab yer known de 'fendant?

Jelly: 'Bout as long as she am now. She nebber was any longer.

Snow: You fust met her at a ball.

Jelly: Dat am kerrect.

Snow: An' she struck you at once—

Seraph: Dat am an untroof. I nebber struck him at all.

Crier: Silence!

Snow: But you was struck wiv—

Jelly: I was nebber struck wiv anyfing at all.

Snow: You beheld her in astonishment, den?

Jelly: No. It was in de ball room.

Snow: I suppose you addressed her?

Jelly: No, she was ready dressed; at any rate, what they call "full-dressed."

Snow: But was there any solemn engagement between yer on dat ebenin'?

Jelly: No; dar was nobody between us at de time. I nebber seed him at all.

Snow: Saw who?

Jelly: Solomon Gagement!

Snow: Did yer indite any poetry to de 'fendant on dat occasion?

Jelly: No; it was on a caramel wrapper.

Snow: An' had you any reason to fink dat she partook ob de same spirit as yerself?

Jelly: Oh, no! dar was no spirits in de place.

Seraph: (*Jumps up.*) How dare you say I had any spirits!

Crier: Silence!

Seraph: I shan't silence! I ain't a gwine to hear deformation ob charackter said about me.

Judge: Yer musn't interrupt de court, defendant. De learned counsel am referrin' to de spirit ob poetry—de genius ob romance—

Seraph: Dar was neider gin nor rum ob any kind at de ball, an' if dar was I hadn't any.

Crier: Silence!

Clerk: De learned judge didn't say so. Yer mus' suppress yer flow ob animal spirits.

Seraph: Dar! Spirits again! I tell yer der was none. It's a berry great un-troof.

Judge: (*Bangs his fist on desk.*) Silence, or I'll kemit yer!

(*Seraphina sits down very much fluttered.*)

Brass: Consider, your honor, the delicate feelings ob my unprotected client. (*Soothes her and fans her with his brief.*)

Snow: Now, Mr. Jellybrain, we'll presume de evidence—did yer accompany de 'fendant home dat night?

Jelly: Yes, I did, sar.

Snow: Wiv her own consent?

Jelly: Certainly.

Snow: Dar, dat will do. I needn't question yer as to de little endearments which usually takes place under such suckamstances, I only wanted the judge an' gentlemen ob de jury to 'stablish de fact ob a mutual agreement. Yer may sit down, Mr. Jellybrain. (*As Jellybrain is about to leave the box, Brass rises.*)

Brass: Stay a little, witness, I have a squestion to put. When yer saw my client home on dat night, was dar any casualty on de road?

Jelly: Annie who?

Brass: Any casualty, surely yer know what that means.

Jelly: Der was nobody else on de road at all.

Brass: Den, I suppose, whilst walking along wiv her yer naturally fell into a reberie?

Jelly: No—I didn't; der was no ribber dar, but I fell into a ditch.
Brass: Dat would cubber you wiv vexation an' disappointment, wouldn't it?
Jelly: It cubbered me wiv duckweed and slush.
Brass: What did de lady do den?
Jelly: She went away an' lef' me by myself.
Brass: Den yer went into a rage, didn't you?
Jelly: No, I went inter de next saloon to scrape de mud off my clothes.
Brass: And you had a glass of liquor in de interim?
Jelly: No, I had it at the bar.
Brass: You's berry obtuse.
Jelly: What does year mean by dat?
Brass: You must hab been born incorrigible.
Jelly: Dat statement am not correct. I was born in Ohio.
Brass: You can sit down. (*They both sit down. Snow rises.*)
Snow: Call Peter Periwinkle.
Crier: Peter Periwinkle.
Police: Peter Periwinkle, come into court.
(*Enter Peter Periwinkle—Policeman escorts him to witness box.*)
Snow: Your name's Peter Periwinkle?
Peter: It am, sir.
Snow: Do yer know de 'fendant Miss Seraphina Sugarplum?
Peter: I does, sir, berry well.
Snow: Does she foller any special employment?
Peter: Yes, sar.
Snow: Ob what nature it?
Peter: She am de servant at de Darktown Hotel.
Snow: Does she bear a good character?
Peter: Oh, yes, sar. Yer should see her workin'. She gets up before daylight, sweeps out de place, washes all de dishes, and makes all de beds, afore anybody else gets up in de morning.
Snow: Am you employed at de same hotel?
Peter: Yes, sar. I am de gentleman dat blacks de boots.
Snow: Well, had yer eber any reason to serpose dat any 'tickular engagement was suspended between de plaintiff an' Miss Seraphina Sugarplum?
Peter: Oh, yes, berry often.
Snow: Did dey eber conduct demselbes when day were alone in any way to lead udder people to fink so?
Peter: I nebber was wiv dem when dey was alone.
Snow: When yer say dat you had reason to fink dey was engaged, what makes yer fink so?
Peter: I saw dem once at de park, an' she ordered him to frow his cigeret away, an' he did it wivout de slightest hesitation, jus' as if dey was married.
Seraph: It wasn't for dat; don't you fink it.
Crier: Silence!

Judge: De defendant will hab de opportunity ob gibing her ebidence at de proper time.

Snow: Did de plaintiff display any eccentricity ob manner at any time on de subject?

Peter: Plenty ob tricks in his manner.

Snow: I mean any aberrations ob mind, any tokens ob de hard struggle goin' on wivin?

Peter: No; it was hard-boiled eggs.

Snow: What kernection was dar bitween hard-boiled eggs an' Miss Seraphina Sugarplum?

Peter: He eat a perdigious number ob hard-boiled eggs, because he said he wanted 'em to lie heabby on his stomack, so dat he should forget de weight ob his heart.

Snow: And do yer consider he was berry pointed in his attention?

Brass: I objects to dat squestion bin' put, your honor.

Judge: On what ground does yer object?

Brass: It am no business ob my learned brudder's to enquire inter de points dat was put to my client. Dis case am not turnin' on point—it am dependin' on facks, an' facks am stubborn fings.

Snow: Den you's a fatk.

Brass: An' you's anudder.

Snow: Dar's gwine ter de trubble ober dis case. Yer mus' be de biggest fool in dis yere court to make such an objection!

Brass: An' you must be de biggest fool in de court to put such a squestion—

Judge: Genelmen! Yer forgets dat I'se here. I allows der squestion ter be put, but I'll take a note ob de objection.

Snow: Den I'll repeat it. Did yer notice any pointed or special attention dat he paid to de lady?

Peter: Yes, sar. He berry often pointed to her. He was like one ob dem comperses dat salers uses—he wanted to show his points on ebery side at once.

Snow: Did she nebber speak ter you about her matrimonial prospecks?

Peter: Yes, sah; she said she was gwine ter hab a fine house wiv a garden, an' a summerhouse wiv a big culprit on de top—

Snow: I presumes yer means a cupola?

Peter: Oh, yes; I knows what I means—an' she said dat de garden was ter be laid out in turpentine walks—

Snow: Serpentine!

Peter: Yes; and dar would be lemonades all round de sides for de illustrated visitors, which would shed—would shed—

Snow: Well?

Peter: Dar was nuffin else. She nebber got any furder dan dat wood-shed.

Snow: Well, dat am sufficient to show to de satisfaction ob de court dat de defendant contemplated de subjeck of matromoney wif my client. I shall now purceed to put de 'fendant into de witness box. Call Seraphina Sugarplum. (*Peter is led out by Policeman.*)

Crier: Syrupina Pluggerthumb!

(*Seraphina rises, but Policeman not being there to conduct her to the witness box, Jellybrain comes forward and gives her his arm.*)

Snow: Your name am Seraphina Sugarplum?

Seraph: Yes; it am; an' I ain't shamed ob it.

Snow: Answer wifout comments, please. I believe you am bound by a solumn contract to de plaintiff?

Seraph: All contracks between me an' Josephus Jellybrain is off.

Judge: You mus' be aware ob de serious nature ob engagements ob dis kind. Do you ebber attend church?

Seraph: Yes, I does, berry often, sometimes—now an' den.

Snow: An' what am your objeck in goin' dar?

Brass: (*Rising.*) I submit ter yer honor dat am no business ob dis court, an' such an inpertinent squestion hab not any right to be asked.

Snow: I shan't insist on de answer, brudder Brass. People goes to church sometimes for berry equivercal purposes, an' if de witness likes ter leabe herself open to anyfing ob dat kind, she may do so.

Brass: Why, what does people allers go to church for?

Snow: Sometimes for fishin'.

Brass: Yes, for husbands. I hopes my learned brudder doesn't insinevate dat my client, a lady ob her 'spectability, hab any sich motib?

Seraph: Don't you fink it. I nebber go fishin' wiv spoon-bait. I goes to church because I likes de *hims*.

Brass: And de hims go 'cos day like de *shes*.

Judge: An' berry proper, too. Yer can get along, brudder Snowball.

Snow: Yer say dat your 'gagement wiv my client am off?

Seraph: Off? Clear off, an' no mistake!

Snow: What reason does yer allege for de breach?

Seraph: For de what!

Snow: De breach. Breaches ob promise am common enuff.

Seraph: His was tweeds.

Snow: His what?

Seraph: His-hem! Dem he had on when we went ter de park.

Snow: Yer honor, I can get nothin' out ob be obstrusity ob dis witness. I can't get a straight answer.

Brass: (*Rises.*) Suppose I tries to do de same wiv her.

Snow: You's welcum. (*Sits down.*)

Brass: Now, Miss Sugarplumb, will you tell me your candid erpinion ob de plaintiff?

Seraph: He am a young man ob great promise.

Brass: In what particular?

Seraph: He hab promised to marry half ob de girls in Darktown.

Brass: Was he in de habit ob writing poetry to dem all?

Seraph: Mostly—some ob dem. He wrote some beautiful verses to Dinah Black lass week.

Brass: Was he making lub to her at de time?

Seraph: Yes, he was; an' half-a-dozen beside.

Judge: Can you repeat does lines?

Seraph: I fink so—

"Her neck am like de ostrich,
Her froat am like de swan,
Her face am like a pumpkin,
Wiv de sun a'shinin' on,
She went to de beach for bathin'
Her complexion den got spiled,
Her cheeks all peeled, and her nose went red,
Like a lobster when it's biled."

Judge: Der am plenty ob force an' expression in de poetry. It am ebident de plaintiff am a jennyass.

Brass: Yer mentioned a certian visit to de park, was de same visit mentioned by de last witness, when yer made plaintiff frow his cigaret away?

Seraph: It was, sir.

Brass: An' why did yer insist on his doin' so? Is it because yer objects ter tobaker, as ladies often does?

Seraph: No; I doesn't object ter tobaker, but I faught he'd be teachin de rest ob de monkeys in de cages bad habits.

Brass: What occurred in de conduct ob de plaintiff ter cause yer ter break off wiv him?

Seraph: A great many fings.

Brass: Can yer give us somefing tangible to lay hold ob?

Seraph: Well, yer might fink ob layin' hold ob his moustache, if it wasn't so much like a base-ball match.

Judge: Why am it like a base-ball match?

Seraph: Why, dar's only nine a side.

Snow: (*Rising.*) Is dat all de objections to my client?

Seraph: Oh, no. He was allers stealin kisses.

Snow: But yer cannot call dat an objection from yer own intended husband.

Seraph: Can't I, when he allers stole 'em from udder girls?

Snow: Oh, ah—um! (*Sits down.*)

Brass: Dat am quite conclusib. Has he ebber behaved bad to yer on any special occasion?

Seraph: Yes, when we was at de park, I asked him ter pin a flower on my buzzum, an' he did it wif such a flourish ob his arm dat he stuck de pin into de end ob my nose, an' made it bleed berry much.

Snow: But dat was only an accident; yer couldn't say dat was a piece ob bad conduct.

Seraph: But when he took de label from a spool ob cotton which he had in his pocket, and put it on de end ob my nose to stop de bleeding, and made my nose read, "Warranted 200 yards long," it was enuff to disgust de sensibilities ob any lady in de world.

Snow: Dat am no justifercation for breaking off an existin' engagement, an' blightin' de life ob my client—a paltry nose scratch.

Brass: I takes objection to de remark, "paltry," as applied ter my client's nose—dar am nuffin paltry about it.

Snow: Her nose am as paltry as her conduct.

Brass: You's anudder!

Judge: Silence!

Brass: You's a feller, brudder Snowball!

Snow: An I repeats it.

Judge: Will yer be quiet? (*Throws his instand at them. The counsel begin to strike each other with their papers. Seraphina faints in the arms of the plaintiff, who takes her to her seat. The Jury come out of their seats and gather round fighting counsel.*)

Judge: (*Coming down from bench.*) If dat's der way you's gwine to settle dis case I shall adjourn de court for luncheon. (*Exit Judge. Counsel and Clerk follow. Jury are about to follow when Policeman stops them.*)

Police: Hold on dar. Dis court don't allow no luncheon for jurymen. Yer mus' return to de jury-box till de case am concluded. I ain't allowed ter let yer go away for a minute. De plaintiff an' defendant am opshunal. (*Jellybrain and Seraphina come forward, as Jury retire into their box again, and shyly approach each other.*)

Seraph: Josephus Jellybrain, how can yer look me in the face?

Jelly: Seraphina, why hab yer broken my heart?

Seraph: Couldn't eben chip it. Why did yer leave off comin' to our house, Josephus?

Jelly: Because you began to learn de piano, Seraphina. A poetic soul can stand a great deal, but to listen to a young lady learnin' de piano am above human endurance.

Jelly: Den return me my presents, Seraphina.

Seraph: You nebber gave me any, Josephus.

Jelly: What! am all my kisses forgotten? All dose confessions ob a divine inspiration?

Seraph: De kisses yer can hab back—yer ungrateful man—any time yer like ter come for them.

Jelly: Well, habin' arranged dat to our mutual satisfaction, we'll adjourn for lunch. (*Offers his arm. Exit arm-in-arm.*)

Police: Now, gentlemen ob de jury, I shall lock de court-room door, an' leab you to consider de verdict. (*Exit Policeman.*)

(*Jury come out of box, and sit about stage.*)

Foreman: What does you say; shall we bring dem in guilty ob manslaughter?

1st Jury: What for?

Fore: For not getting married.

2nd Jury: De plaintiff am guilty.

Fore: What ob?

2nd Jury: Ob not knowing when he's well off.

3rd Jury: I say de woman am de worst.

4th Jury: An' I say it's de man. It's allers de man in dese cases.

5th Jury: Dat am an untroof.

Fore: Now, gentlemen, I shall fine yer all for mutiny an' insubordination.

6th Jury: I don't care what yer does, I's not gwine to hear de woman run down.

3rd Jury: An' I'll not hear de men belied.

4th Jury: (*Throws a law-book at him.*) Dat soon settles de squestion. (*Here they begin to throw the papers and books from the tables at each other. In the midst of the confusion the Policeman enters.*)

Police: Stop! stop! De case am settled. De plaintiff an' defendant hab eloped togedder, an' his honor invites yer all ter luncheon.

(*They all rush to the door, and after a deal of pushing and struggling for precedence, they all get out.*)

(*Curtain.*)

THREE O'CLOCK TRAIN
(A Vaudeville Version Collected by Douglas Gilbert)

CAST: Comic. Straight

SETTING: A bare and dingy room.

STRAIGHT: If I didn't have this handout here I don't know what I'd do. I get the place rent free because the landlord thinks it is haunted. (*Inevitable knock.*) Come in. (*Enter Comic.*)

COMIC: (*Exaggerated Negro dialect.*) Good mawnin'. I just stopped in for some information.

STRAIGHT: I'll try to accommodate you. What is it?

COMIC: What time does the three o'clock train go out?

STRAIGHT: The three o'clock train? Why, it goes out exactly sixty minutes past two o'clock.

COMIC: That's funny. The man at the station told me it went out exactly sixty minutes before four o'clock.

STRAIGHT: Well, you won't miss your train anyway.

COMIC: No, well, I'm much obliged. (*Exits.*)

STRAIGHT: Curious sort of chap. (*Picks up banjo and strums quietly as Comic re-enters.*)

COMIC: Excuse me, which is the other side of the street?

STRAIGHT: Why, the other side of the street is just across the way.

COMIC: That's funny. I asked the fellow across the street and he said it was over here.

STRAIGHT: Well, you can't depend on everything you hear.

COMIC: No, that's so.

STRAIGHT: Well, you've got plenty of time to make your train. Sit down a while.

COMIC: (*Seating himself, and scanning the wretched room.*) Nice place you have here. Nice comfortable place.

STRAIGHT: Yes, I get the place for a very reasonable rent. Know why I get it so cheaply?

COMIC: You don't pay the rent.

STRAIGHT: No, no. It's because the place is haunted. (*Comic looks around uneasily.*)

STRAIGHT: But you're not afraid of ghosts?

COMIC: Oh, no. I'm not afraid of ghosts. My grandmother used to keep a ghost boardinghouse. Some of my best friends are ghosts. (*Looks nervously around.*)

STRAIGHT: Well, I'm glad to hear that because this house is full of ghosts.

COMIC: When do the, that is, when, er, where are they, these er . . . ?

STRAIGHT: Oh, they're liable to come in any time.

COMIC: (*Shuddering.*) Right in here?

STRAIGHT: Oh, yes, right in here. They just waft in and waft right out again.

COMIC: They, they waft, do they? (*Looks around uneasily.*)

STRAIGHT: What's the matter?

COMIC: I thought something was wafting.

STRAIGHT: Well, you wouldn't care, would you?

COMIC: (*With exaggeration.*) Oh, no. I wouldn't care.

STRAIGHT: Like to hear a good song?

COMIC: Yes, I always liked music. Something lively.

STRAIGHT: All right, I'll sing you a good lively song.

COMIC: Something to cheer us up?

STRAIGHT: Oh, yes. Something very cheerful. (*Sings, in dismal wail:*)

> The old jawbone on the alms house wall.
> It hung fifty years on that whitewashed wall.
> It was grimy and gray, and covered with gore,
> Like the souls of the sinners who'd passed there before.
> Chorus: Oh, the old jawbone, the jawbone, etc.

(*Chains rattle and weird noises are heard backstage as stage lights dim. Comic shivers in terror.*)

STRAIGHT: What's the matter with you?

COMIC: Oh, nothing. Nothing at all. I'm just enjoying the music. That's a nice lively song.

STRAIGHT: Oh, wait till you hear the second verse. (*Sings, still in dismal wail:*)
>   At twelve o'clock near the hour of one,
>   A figure appears that will strike you dumb.
>   He grabs you by the hair of the head,
>   And he grabs you about until you are dead.

(*Offstage noises and wails. Straightman rises and ghost enters and straightman exits, singing.*)
>   Oh, the old jawbone . . .

(*Ghost slithers to chair vacated by Straightman and sits beside Comic unknown to him because he has not seen the entrance.*)

COMIC: (*Still unaware of ghost.*) Why not sing something we both know? We'll sing it together. Yours is a good song but I don't like the way it ends. (*Ghost nudges Comic.*)

COMIC: I wasn't asleep. I was just listening to the music. Is it most time for them ghosts to waft? (*He looks casually to one side and sees part of the white sheet. He follows his glance, takes in ghost completely, and rises, horrified, as ghost rises with him. He pulls the string of fright wig and hair stands straight up. Recovering somewhat, Comic edges away and then dashes round stage, and ghost, his finger pointing at Comic, pursues. As Ghost gradually gains on Comic, Comic exits, diving through breakaway window.*)

PETE IN THE WELL
Jack Roach's Version

CAST: Jake. Straight. Pete.
SETTING: A Pawnshop.

STRAIGHT: I'm *most* annoyed tonight! I forgot to lock my safe last night and I have just discovered that someone has stolen twelve cents out of the safe. An old dime and two pennies. Keepsakes. I'll call Jake and Pete and I'll bet I'll get to the bottom of this! Jake! Come up here!

JAKE: (*Enters.*) Yas'm (or Yassir).

STRAIGHT: (*Repeats what happened and asks.*) Now, what I want to know is DO YOU KNOW WHAT HAPPENED TO MY OLD COINS?!

(*Jake denies—Straight presses—Jake denies until finally he yields by saying, "If you don't tell him I told you, I'll tell you."—Looks offstage both directions, then sidles up to Straight and in a hoarse whisper says, "Last night I went to the carnival and I saw Pete and his girl friend. They were licking a 1¢ lollipop each and riding on the 5¢ merry-go-round. So there goes your 12¢."*)

STRAIGHT: Aha! I thought so! I'll just call him up here and fire him!

JAKE: Let me outta here first!

STRAIGHT: No! You stay here! (*Turns and calls.*) Pete!

PETE: (*Offstage—in a surly, rough voice.*) What do you want?

STRAIGHT: Come up here right away—it's very important!

PETE: I'll come when I get good and ready!

STRAIGHT: You'll come NOW!

PETE: (*Enters, and again says.*) OK, I'm here. What do you want?

STRAIGHT: I understand you were on the merry-go-round with your girl last night. Where did you get the money?

PETE: Who told you I was on the merry-go-round?

STRAIGHT: A little bird told me.

PETE: Oh, yeah? I'll bet it was a damned BLACK Bird! (*Starts running after Jake menacingly. Jake flees all round the Straight, as he yells, "Hold 'im! Hold 'im!" When Straight DOES hold Pete, Jake takes up a sparring stance and says, "Let 'im go! I ain't scared of 'im! Let 'im go!" Straight lets Pete go and Jake turns tail, again yelling, "Hold 'im!" This is done two or three times. Then Straight says, "Enough of this! Pete, you're fired!"*)

PETE: (*Aside to audience.*) Too damned late, I quit ten minutes ago—(*Exits.*) I'm coming back to rob this joint tonight.

JAKE: Did you hear that? Did you hear what he said?

STRAIGHT: No—what did he say?

JAKE: (*In awed amazement—wide-eyed*) He said he's coming back to rob this joint tonight.

STRAIGHT: He DID, did he! Well—we'll just see about that. I never did like that guy anyway. Now, Jake, here's what we will do—you hide over there and I'll hide over here. You take the broom and hit him over the head if you have to. I'll take the gun, and we'll just lay for him. (*They hide in opposite wings.*)

(*Enter Pete—stealthily creeping, looking to right and left. Pulls drawer out of table as Jake comes up behind with brush end of broom and swats him just as the Straight fires the gun. Pete falls flat on his back with his arms and legs outstretched.*)

JAKE: Lordy! You done killed him!

STRAIGHT: I didn't kill him, Jake. You did. (*While Jake is protesting his innocence, Straight removes broom and puts gun in Jake's hand.*) I had the broom, YOU shot him!

JAKE: No siree—I had the broom—Yi! How did I get that thing?! (*Gingerly lays gun on table and backs away.*)

STRAIGHT: Jake, we've got to move fast. Now that you've killed him, the Pinkerton detectives will be after you.

JAKE: Oh, Lordy, I don't want no Pink-eyed detectives after me!

STRAIGHT: Well, here's what we must do, then. We will get rid of the body, then take inventory and run away to Canada. That's our only chance!

JAKE: OK. What do you want me to do?

STRAIGHT: Get rid of the body.

JAKE: How I gonna do dat?

STRAIGHT: There's an old well in the backyard. Uncover it—throw him in— throw in a lot of rocks, then cover it back. Hurry! We haven't got a minute to lose. (*Exits.*)

JAKE: Oh, Lordy, I gotta get rid of the body. Look at that son of a gun! Died jest like a pair of scissors—all spread out. OK, here goes. (*He pulls feet together and Pete's arms fly straight up. Jake jumps back in fright. Then he stands astride Pete and pushes his arms back down to his sides. Pet's feet fly up, kicking Jake in the buttocks. Jake jumps away in fright again. Finally he pushes Pete's feet to the floor again, causing Pete to sit up. Jake adjusts Pete so that he is facing the audience. Then he sits down by Pete and apologizes, saying—"I swear, Pete, I didn't shoot you. I'm sorry about the whole mess." As he talks, Pete slowly turns his head and looks at Jake who discovers the staring eyes and pushes the head back around to the front. Repeat. Then Jake goes and sits on the other side. Pete turns that way. Repeat. Finally Jake says, "OK, I gotta get rid of the body." He puts his arms under Pete's arms, lifts him to a standing position, and bounces him along to the side of the stage where he carefully props him against a wing. In bouncing Pete, Jake loses his hat—it falls just out of reach. He tries to pick it up, but Pete teeters forward, about to fall. Repeat. Finally, Jake lies down on his back, holding up the teetering Pete with his feet. Jake grabs his hat and puts it on. Jake gets up, turns his back to Pete, and reaches over his shoulders to carry him on his back. Pete ducks down. As Jake turns to look at him, Pete stands straight again. Repeat. The third time, Pete escapes off the stage. Jake yells for Straight, "Hey, Boss! Hey, Boss!"*)

STRAIGHT: Well, Jake, I see you got rid of the body.

JAKE: (*Bewildered—looking around worriedly.*) Yas'm—I got rid of the body, all right.

STRAIGHT: Now, Jake, you sit here at the table and take this tablet and pencil and write down what I call off to you.

JAKE: But I can't see! It's dark in here.

STRAIGHT: Well, then, light a candle. (*Exits. Jake lights the candle, which is already sitting on the table. The table is covered to the floor with a cloth and a fourth person is under the table manipulating the spooky candle. The Straight calls from offstage.*) "Three Chickering Pianos."

(*Jake writes laboriously as he mutters, "Three chickens on a Piano," then watches in fascinated horror as the candle "grows" taller and taller and taller. He yells, "Hey Boss!" Straight enters.*)

STRAIGHT: What's the matter, Jake?

(*Jake blubbers at the now normal-size candle. Straight fusses a little and exits as Jake sits down again.*)

STRAIGHT: (*From offstage.*) "Seventeen monkey wrenches."

JAKE: "Seventeen wenches." (*Then Jake watches the candle slide across the table. He calls the Straight. The candle returns to its place. The Straight fusses, then says, "Jake bring the candle over here and let me see what you've written down." Jake brings the candle.*)

STRAIGHT: Hold it so I can see. (*Pause.*) Higher. Higher, Jake. (*Jake now looks like the Statue of Liberty, with his arm fully extended over his head. Straight looks up and says, "Oh, Jake, LOWER!" Jake lowers it below reading level. Straight says, "Lower! Lower!" looks up and says, "Jake! Hold it betwixt and between!" Jake turns back to audience, bends over and holds candle flame to seat of pants, then jumps and howls in pain. Straight finally gets Jake's hand in the correct position and says.)*

"Jake! Who said anything about chickens on a piano?

JAKE: You did. You was right in dat room over there *(extends arm)* when you said it.

(Ghost enters, puts head under arm and looks at Jake. Jake pantomimes fear, then slowly looks at ghost—clamps arm down hysterically, dropping candle as he beats himself on the arm. The ghost has escaped.)

STRAIGHT: What's the matter with you, Jake?

JAKE: I saw him—Pete. Right here!

STRAIGHT: Stop the nonsense. We have no time to lose. Get with it, man! What else did you write? Oh, Jake! I never said anything like this! I said MONKEY wrenches.

(Ghost crawls in. Jake's legs are spread wide enough for the ghost to lie down on his back looking up at Jake as he snatches and pulls Jake's pants legs repeatedly. Jake has trouble keeping his pants on and holding the candle. He sees the ghost, who escapes. Jake sits down violently where the ghost had been. Straight fusses. Jake gets up. Straight gives Jake the paper and says, "We'll do the rest of it now, but this must be done over." The ghost comes in again and taps Straight on the shoulder, then points offstage. The terrified Straight exits silently. Jake is still arguing—"You was right over there, etc." Ghost in somber tones quavers, "It's all wrong.")

JAKE: You got a cold or sumpin, Boss? Your voice sure changed sudden-like!

(Jake slowly looks around at the ghost, then runs offstage with the ghost riding on his back.)

OVER THE RIVER, CHARLIE
Anna Mae Noell's Version

CAST:

Dr. Kelly (doting, protective father)

Kitty Kelly (his beautiful daughter)

Kitty's Suitor, "Charlie"

The Houseboy, "Jake"

SETTING: The Living Room of Kelly's Home

DR. KELLY: *(Pacing the floor, anxiously, muttering)* I'M SURE LITTLE WILLIE GREEN DIED OF WATER ON THE BRAIN! If only he could have been autopsied. What a sinful waste. Now we'll never know! I know what I'll do! I'll get Jake to bring the body up here and no one will know the difference. An inspiration! Positively the only solution! Why didn't I think of it before! Jake! Oh, Jake! Come here, please!

JAKE: Yass suh, doc, here I is.

DR. KELLY: Jake, how would you like to make $5.00?

JAKE: Who I gotta kill?

DR. KELLY: You won't have to kill anybody, Jake. Just run a very important errand for me and promise not to tell a soul.

JAKE: O.K., sounds good. What I gotta do?

DR. KELLY: Jake, do you remember little Willie Green?

JAKE: Yessuh, I owes him 50¢.

DR. KELLY: Well, Jake, Willie Green died this morning and was buried this afternoon. I want you to go to the cemetery and bring the body here.

JAKE: I just remembered—I forgot sumpin.

DR. KELLY: What did you forget?

JAKE: I forgot to stay home while I was there. (*Starts to go.*)

DR. KELLY: (*Grabs him—pulls him to center stage and talks confidently.*) Jake, if you do a good job I'll not only give you the $5.00 but I'll throw in a gallon of gin.

JAKE: I'm your man!

DR. KELLY: OK, Jake, here's a big canvas bag. You bring him back in that. Do you know how to get to the cemetery?

JAKE: No suh—I ain't got no business in no cemetery. Sho' don't.

DR. KELLY: OK, Jake, when you leave the house, turn left. Keep walking until you come to a fork in the road.

JAKE: Who lost de fork?

DR. KELLY: No, Jake—two roads—one goes this way and the other goes that way. I want you to take up the road to the right.

JAKE: (*Throws bag at Doctor.*) How de Hell I gonna do that? I cain't TAKE UP NO ROAD!

DR. KELLY: No, Jake, you don't understand—you WALK up the road.

JAKE: Gimme the bag.

DR. KELLY: Then you'll come to the river. You'll see a rowboat there. Untie the boat and PULL UP the river!

JAKE: (*Throws bag.*) I cain't pull up no river!

DR. KELLY: No, no, no, Jake—you ROW up the river.

JAKE: OK, gimme the bag.

DR. KELLY: When you get to the other side you'll see a high stone wall.

JAKE: The Plenny tenchery.

DR. KELLY: No, Jake, the cemetery wall.

JAKE: (*Throws bag.*) I ain't got no business round no cemetery.

DR. KELLY: Jake, remember the $5.00.

JAKE: I don't need no $5.00.

DR. KELLY: Don't forget the gin!

JAKE: Gimme the bag!

DR. KELLY: Now when you walk over to the wall you'll see a tall ladder lying there. You put the ladder to the wall, climb up to the top and . . .

JAKE: (Throws bag.) Yeah, and some son of a gun yanks dat ladder away and there I'll be!

DR. KELLY: No one will be there to bother you. They're all dead.

JAKE: Dat's why I ain't goin!

DR. KELLY: Remember the $5.00.

JAKE: Nemind the $5.00.

DR. KELLY: The gin?

JAKE: Gimme the bag!

DR. KELLY: Now, once you get into the cemetery, you walk *past* two vaults on your right. The third one, you go in. Remove the lid from the first coffin. Feel the face. That's an old man with a long beard. That's not the man we want.

JAKE: Dat ain't de man we want.

DR. KELLY: Replace the lid, then check the next coffin. That's a lady with long hair . . .

JAKE: Dat ain't de man we want.

DR. KELLY: In the third coffin is little Willie Green . . .

JAKE: (*Throws bag.*) Take de bag. Just about dat time Willie gwine rise up and say, "Gimme dat 50¢ you owe me, boy." I ain't goin.

DR. KELLY: Remember the $5.00.

JAKE: Done told ya, don't need no $5.00.

DR. KELLY: Don't forget the gin!

JAKE: Gimme the bag.

DR. KELLY: OK now, you hurry and bring him up here and you'll get the gallon of gin and $5.00 too. (*Jake exits. Doctor paces a little more in self-satisfaction.*) I'd better go make preparations for the autopsy. (*Exits.*)

(*Curtain.*)

(*Enter Charlie in front of curtain.*)

CHARLIE: (*Thinking aloud.*) I don't know how we can do it, but Kitty and I want to get married. Her father won't give his consent so we must elope. I've got to come up with a plan tonight or she may be too frightened to do it. (*Exits.*)

(*Curtain.*)

(*Jake is onstage with a still form stretched out on the operating table.*)

JAKE: Doc—oh, Doc! I'm back.

DR. KELLY: (*Enters. Shows elated surprise.*) My, that was fast work, Jake. You stay here now and keep an eye on him and I'll be right back to pay you.(*Exits.*)

JAKE: (*Almost panics when the "corpse" sits up and turns out to be Charlie.*) How'd *you* get in dat bag?

CHARLIE: Remember when you stopped to rest at the foot of the hill? Well, I took Willie out and I got in.

JAKE: You mean you let me carry you all the way up that hill? I'm gonna tell the Doc.

CHARLIE: No, Jake, Kitty and I plan to elope tonight. It was the only way I could safely enter the house. Now you've got to help us.

JAKE: How can I do that?

CHARLIE: You can lie on the table until we get back.

JAKE: No suh—he's gonna do a cuttin' job on de corpse. I ain't gonna be no corpse.

CHARLIE: He won't autopsy until tomorrow.

JAKE: Well, OK. But what if something goes wrong?

CHARLIE: I won't be far away. You just yell out, "Over the river, Charlie," and I'll be RIGHT HERE. (*Exits as Jake lies down.*)

DR. KELLY: (*Offstage. Yells.*) This is what I'll use to cut out his diaphragm. (*Throws a carpenter's hand saw onto the stage.*)

JAKE: Charlie! "Over the river, Charlie!"

CHARLIE: (*Enters quickly.*) What is it, Jake?

JAKE: (*Pointing to the saw.*) DAT's what he's gonna use to cut out my fryin' pan.

CHARLIE: Jake, I told you. He won't do anything until tomorrow. Do be quiet! (*Exits.*)

DR. KELLY: (*Offstage.*) This is my scalpel. (*He throws a big butcher knife on the stage.*)

JAKE: Charlie! "Over the river, Charlie!"

CHARLIE: (*Reenters.*) Now what?

JAKE: (*Points at the knife.*) He says he gonna SCALP HELL outta me!

CHARLIE: Not until tomorrow. Jake, be quiet! (*He exits on one side as Dr. Kelly enters on the other.*)

DR. KELLY: Aha—alone at last! (*He lifts the cover from the face and jumps back in surprise.*) I do believe half the proof is right here, right now, that I was right. The corpse is turning black already! Dear me! This means I can't wait till tomorrow. Let's see, I guess I'll start at this end. (*Indicates the head. The doctor turns around and bends over to pick up a tool. As he does, Jake hastily switches ends. The doctor raises up the cover and sees the feet where the head had been seconds before.*) Dear me! I've worried so much over this I'm afraid I'm losing my mind. I could have sworn the head was *here* a moment ago. Oh, well. I can work on his feet first, it really doesn't matter. (*He turns, bends over to exchange a tool, and Jake switches ends again. Doctor sees that the feet are gone and the head is back. He walks toward the footlights.*) Something is very strange here. (*Charlie and Kitty come onstage.*)

KITTY: (*Hugs father.*) Oh, Daddy, Charlie and I just got married.

DR. KELLY: Well, since it's already done, I'll give you my blessing. (*He takes their right hands, holds them high over his head.*) May your first year be happiness and your second year joy . . .

JAKE: (*Jumps up behind them.*) . . . And the third year a girl, and the fourth a boy.

CLUCK'S SANITARIUM SCENE

CAST: Comic. Straight. Juvenile. Ingenue.

SET: Doctor's office. Examining table. Desk and chair. Doctor's utensils.

OPENING: Doctor discovered at desk; orderly enters.

Orderly: Oh, Doctor.

Doctor: What is it?

Orderly: There's a YOUNG MAN outside fussing with the Girl. He says his name is LUKE THATCHER. And he wants to see the doctor.

Doctor: Very well; send him in. (*Orderly exits.*)

Luke: (*Sticks his head in door.*) Anybody home?

Doctor: No.

Luke: Well, there's no use me coming in. (*Doc calls him in*). Are you DR. CUTTEM?

Doctor: Yes, that's me. Where are you from?

Luke: San . . . San . . . San . . .

Doctor: San Francisco?

Luke: Chicago.

Doctor: Tell me, Luke, are there any more at home like you?

Luke: Oh, sure. Four . . . Four . . . Four . . .

Doctor: Four?

Luke: Fourteen.

Doctor: Tell me, Luke, do you smoke?

Luke: Oh, yeh. I smoke Boo . . . Boo . . . Boo . . . DUKES MIXTURE.

Doctor: I suppose you want work?

Luke: Yes, if I can't find anything else to do.

Doctor: Well, come with me. I will show you what I want you to do. NOW, this is the OPERATING TABLE.

Luke: I see you have the TABLE all set. I'll be seeing you. (*Starts to exit.*)

Doctor: Here, Luke, where are you going?

Luke: My mother's got a boy down at our house she don't care a darn about. I'll send him up.

Doctor: Luke, you're not AFRAID?

Luke: No, I'm just SCARED I'll be AFRAID. I'm going to get on that TABLE?

Doctor: I hope YOU are.

Luke: I HOPE I AIN'T.

Doctor: Why LUKE, you have nothing to FEAR. You see what that is on the TABLE? That is a CADAVER. Constructed from different parts of people I have OPERATED ON.

Luke: DIFFERENT HUNKS OF PEOPLE?

Doctor: Well, have it your own way. I want you to get on the TABLE and take HIS PLACE.

Luke: Oh, no. I don't want to be a CADAVER.

Doctor: Listen, LUKE. I know a LADY, I'm very much in LOVE with. Now if I can make HER believe that I can bring that DUMMY back to LIFE, SHE will MARRY ME. Now all you do is get on the TABLE, I will give YOU some OXYGEN and ELECTRICITY, YOU breathe heavily, and SHE will think I brought YOU back to LIFE, then SHE will MARRY ME. WE'LL GET MARRIED.

Luke: What did you say?

Doctor: I said: WE'LL GET MARRIED.

Luke: Oh, no. MY MOTHER told ME never to MARRY A MAN.

Doctor: I mean the LADY.

Luke: Oh, oh. That's different.

Doctor: NOW, when you get on the TABLE . . .

Luke: You mean, IF I get on that TABLE.

Doctor: Come on LUKE, hurry and get on the TABLE. Take hold of the DUMMY and carry it into the BATHROOM. YOU have nothing to FEAR, LUKE. I want you to go in there now, put on a pair of PAJAMAS and fix up to look like a DUMMY. (Bus.). Just a moment LUKE, the PHONE is ringing. (Takes phone.) Yes, Mamm.

Luke: Shall I keep MY PANTS ON?

Doctor: No, take your pants off. (Bus.). I beg your pardon, that was a mistake on MY part. I was INTERRUPTED. You see, WE were preparing for a MAJOR OPERATION. I am about to CUT out a MAN'S GEMFAC-TICS, also HIS MILADILA. Alright, yes, I will attend to that right away. Yes. Good bye.

Luke: Oh, Doc. I don't want MY, what you said, CUT OUT.

Doctor: Say, do you know that YOU nearly got ME in trouble?

Luke: Say, Doc, who was that on the phone?

Doctor: THAT was the LADY I was telling YOU about. Now go in there and put on the PAJAMAS. Remember: try and look like a DUMMY. That shouldn't be too hard. (Luke muggs this up and exits into room.)

Nurse: (Enters down left stage.) Oh, Doctor. (Goes to door where Luke entered.)

Doctor: Yes, what do you want DEAR? (Nurse tries door. It is locked.)

Nurse: Why have YOU got this DOOR LOCKED?

Doctor: OH, IS THAT DOOR LOCKED?

Nurse: NOW, DOCTOR. YOU'RE UP TO SOMETHING. WHAT IS IT? I WANT TO KNOW.

Doctor: I was just making PREPARATIONS for an OPERATION.

Nurse: Doctor, are you really going to try to bring that DUMMY to LIFE?

Doctor: I CERTAINLY AM.

Nurse: BUT DOCTOR, YOU can't do that.

Doctor: Nevertheless, DEAR, I'M going to try. And if I am SUCCESSFUL, I will expect YOU to keep YOUR PROMISE.

Nurse: And will it have the WHOOPING COUGH? And the MEASLES? ETC. . . .

Doctor: NO. It will have the BODY of a MAN, but the BRAIN of a CHILD.

Nurse: OH, I SEE. Well, when you are ready for the OPERATION, just let me know. (*Exit.*)

Luke: (*Offstage.*) OH, DOCTOR, DOCTOR.

Doctor: WELL, what is it?

Luke: I can't get into these SLIPPERS.

Doctor: What's the matter? Are they too SMALL?

Luke: NOPE.

Doctor: TOO LARGE?

Luke: NOPE.

Doctor: WELL, what's the matter with them?

Luke: I CAN'T FIND THEM. (*Enters in pajamas.*)

Doctor: LUKE, you look splendid. You don't know how much you look like a DUMMY.

Luke: YEH, I FEEL LIKE A DUMMY.

Doctor: Now if you get on the TABLE, I will explain . . .

Luke: I'd just as soon stand HERE.

Doctor: You MUST get on the TABLE.

Luke: I don't mind getting on there. BUT TELL ME, is there anyone up here with me.

Doctor: CERTAINLY NOT. Now I want to COVER you up.

Luke: I'M NOT COLD.

Doctor: WHY, what's the matter?

Luke: I don't want nothin in MY way. Hey DOC see that BEND in the road out there? (*Doc says yes.*) Well, when I leave here, I'M going to straighten it out.

Doctor: You have nothing to FEAR. I'll be with you all the time.

Luke: DOC if you are, you're going to be running like the DEVIL.

Doctor: You notice all these fine little wires running around the TABLE?

Luke: ARE THOSE WIRES?

Doctor: YES. They carry the CURRENTS of JUICE.

Luke: Oh, JUICY CURRANTS.

Doctor: They are connected with the SWITCHBOARD. They carry 10,000 VOLTS OF ELECTRICITY into YOUR BODY.

Luke: I WANT MY PANTS.

Doctor: YOU can't have your PANTS until this is entirely all over with.

Luke: I want my PANTS before it is over with.

Doctor: YOU have nothing to FEAR. I am going to HANDLE the ELECTRICITY. I'll see that YOU don't get too much.

Luke: SAY, DOC, when will YOU know when I get too much?

Doctor: YOU know LUKE, I never thought of that.

Luke: It's a pretty darn good idea to think of it.

Doctor: I have it. When YOU have enuf, you raise your right arm, and I'll cut it off.

Luke: CUT IT OFF.

Doctor: THE ELECTRICITY. (*Nurse calls off stage.*) Hurry up now, get on the TABLE. Here SHE comes. Don't forget, that YOU are a DUMMY. (*Luke gets on table.*)

Luke: SHE'LL know what I am when SHE looks at ME.

Nurse: (*Enters.*) ALL READY for the OPERATION, DOCTOR?

Doctor: ALL READY NURSE.

Nurse: AND have you full control of the OXYGEN?

Doctor: FULL control of the OXYGEN.

Nurse: FULL control of the ELECTRICITY?

Doctor: FULL control of the ELECTRICITY. NOW you may assist me by holding this close to the NOSTRILS. (*Bus. with Doc and Luke.*) ARE YOU READY?

Nurse: ALL READY DOCTOR. (*She sees Luke move.*) Oh, oh, Doctor . . . (*She falls in Doctor's arms in semi-faint. She revives. Looks at Luke.*)

Doctor: HE LIVES. HE LIVES. (*Takes nurse out. Luke has leg raised.*) Luke, put down that leg.

Luke: I can't get the DARN thing down.

Doctor: (*Turns off electricity.*) There.

Luke: GIVE ME MY PANTS.

Doctor: YOU can't have your PANTS. (*Bus. Luke on table.*) NOW what is the matter?

Luke: WHO was TICKLING ME? (*Gets off table.*)

Doctor: NO ONE WAS TICKLING YOU. THAT was the ELECTRICITY. It's all over now. YOU don't get any more ELECTRICITY. Get on the TABLE, and don't forget you're a BABY.

Nurse: (*Offstage.*) Oh, Doctor, open this DOOR. I want to see the BABY.

Doctor: YOU can't see the BABY just yet. He hasn't anything on but BANDAGES.

Nurse: I want to give him a bath.

Doctor: WHAT.

Luke: OH, DOC, let HER give ME a BATH.

Nurse: DOCTOR, OPEN THIS DOOR.

Doctor: Just a MINUTE. (*Goes over, opens door.*) COME RIGHT IN MY DEAR.

Nurse: OH, the little precious. I just know I'M going to love him (*Pets baby.*)

Doctor: HERE, HERE, BE CAREFUL. HE'S VERY DELICATE.

Luke: OH, I am not.

Doctor: Shut up.

Nurse: WHAT DID YOU SAY?

Doctor: SEE HOW HE SITS UP? (*Bus.*)

Nurse: OH, I SEE. I know what I'LL do. I'LL go in the other room and get everything ready. I'LL be right back. (*She exits in room where Luke's changed clothes.*)

Doctor: BUT LISTEN DEAR, this child doesn't need a BATH.

Nurse: OH, YES HE DOES. And I'M going to take care of HIM. (*Exits.*)

Doctor: NOW LISTEN YOU. Don't forget that YOU'RE A BABY.

Luke: DIDN'T I DO PRETTY GOOD?

Doctor: YOU did fairly well, BUT YOU didn't say anything.

Luke: WELL, BABIES ain't supposed to say anything.

Doctor: YOU might have CRIED, and said GOO GOO or DA DA. Just to be natural.

Luke: YOU JUST LET HER COME BACK. DOC I'LL CRY, AND SAY GOO GOO, DA DA. . . .

Doctor: SHE isn't coming back, if I can help it. I've had enuf of this. (*Exits.*)

Luke: This JOB ain't so bad after all.

Nurse: (*Enters from upper room.*) THERE, THERE, DARLING.

Luke: GOO, GOO, GOO, DA, DA, DA. . . .

Nurse: OH, isn't HE the SWEETEST little thing. Come, DEAR, and I'LL take care of you.

Luke: GOO GOO. MOMMY. GOO GOO.

Nurse: COME, DEAR. (*They exit in upper room ad libbing.*)

Doctor: (*Enters all excited.*) I wonder where SHE is; I can't find HER ANYWHERE. (*Goes upstage to door.*) OPEN THIS DOOR.

Nurse: DOCTOR. YOU'RE EXCITED. WHAT DO YOU WANT?

Doctor: What have YOU been doing in there with that BABY?

Nurse: WHY, I'VE been CHANGING MY DRESS.

Doctor: NOT CHANGING YOUR DRESS IN FRONT OF THAT BABY?

Nurse: WHY, of course, SILLY, HE'S nothing but a BABY.

Doctor: OPEN THIS DOOR, I SAY. IMMEDIATELY. DO YOU UNDERSTAND. IMMEDIATELY.

Nurse: OH, BE PATIENT, DOCTOR. I'LL OPEN THE DOOR. (*Opens door. Luke sticks out head.*)

Luke: GOO GOO, DA DA.

(*Blackout.*)

DOT QUIED LOTGINGS
A DUTCH SKETCH
(In One Scene)

SCENE: Room in Peter Schlaginhauffen's house. Door in L.F., doors S.E.B. and S.E.L., table B.C., chair each side of table, lounge, L.C., bench upper corner R. Chairs and stools about stage. Peter discovered sitting by table, R.C., reading a paper.

Peter: (*Looking up.*) Py shiminy! dot vos de kind of dings for me. (*Reading.*) "Lotgings wanted by a quiet family in a quiet street. The gentleman of the family is constantly away. The lady spends her evenings at a theatre and sleeps at a hotel. In order to avoid disturbing the people of the house, the children are kept at a boarding school. When the servant girl cleans out the rooms she does so in another house; and the cat has been provided with rubber shoes in order that she may make no noise in going up and down stairs. The dog has been sold in consequence of the high rate of dog tax." (*Striking paper.*) Now, dot vos de sort of beoples to have in a house. But dis dings vos doo good to be drue. (*Looking at paper again.*) It's de pest shoak I efer hear, anyway. (*Coming down.*) Efer since I keep lotging house I have noding but drouble; more droubles as rent. Von man he dend vos bay me for dree months, und don run away; anodder he die mit de small pox. Dot voman mit de vooden leg she vear oud all my carpet und den steal de sheets und pillow gases for me. (*Pausing.*) I nefer did like beoples mit vooden legs. Hans Breitmann haf a vooden leg, und he nefer bay me dot den cents he vos borrow vonce. Vell now, von dings vos certain, nopody mit kinder gomes into dis house; und dem as does gome bays in advance. (*Knock, door R.F.*) Who dos vot, I wonder? Gome in. (*Knock again.*) Gome in, I say! Dot peoples must be deaf. (*A series of very loud knocks.*) Donner und blitzen! vos you want to knock de door in? (*Knock repeated.*) Hol euch der stock schwere noth! Dot vos too much. (*Rushes to door, R.F.*)

(*Enter Mr. Blimber, hurriedly, running against Peter.*)

Blim: (*Staggering back.*) Good gracious! I've fractured my diaphragm.

Peter: (*Roughly.*) Vell, vot you vos vant, anyvays?

Blim: (*Putting up his eyeglass.*) Ah! deah me, ya-a-s.

Peter: Py Gott! he act shust like a monkey.

Blim: (*Bowing extravagantly.*) Are you the landlord?

Peter: (*Imitating him.*) Ya-a-h.

Blim: Ah-h-h!

(*Begins bowing; Peter does the same; they gradually approach one another, until their heads meet with considerable force. Mr. Blimber starts back, rubbing his head.*)

Peter: Now, look here, mine frent, dot vos enough of his foolishness; vot for you vos hammer so at mine front door, eh?

Blim: (*Aside.*) A perfect bear! (*Aloud.*) I did not knock at your door sir.

Peter: Ach was!

Blim: I did not, I assure you.

Peter: Vot vos de use of delling me such a dings? Who it vos den?

Blim: I really do not know, sir.

Peter: Vell, vot you vos vant, anyvays?

Blim: I am looking for a lodging house, sir.

Peter: (*Suddenly realizing.*) Oh! if dot vos de case, sir, you vos gome to de right blace; sit down, (*offers chair*) sit down. (*Mr. Blimber carefully dusts chair with his handkerchief.*) Ach was! sit down.

(*Peter seizes Mr. Blimber by the shoulders, and forces him violently into the chair.*)

Blim: (*Rising.*) But, my dear sir—

Peter: (*Pushing him down.*) Sit down!

Blim: (*Rising.*) But my—

Peter: (*As before.*) Ach was!

Blim: (*Despairingly.*) Great heavens! why, the man is a perfect demon. (*Sinking back into chair.*)

Peter: (*Sitting beside him.*) Now sir, we vos dalk business.

Blim: (*Nervously.*) Ya-a-a-s.

Peter: You vos vant a room?

Blim: Ya-a-a-s.

Peter: (*Eagerly.*) A front room?

Blim: Ya-a-a-s.

Peter: (*Growing excited.*) Mit a pig ped?

Blim: Ya-a-s; exactly.

Peter: (*Slapping him violently on knee.*) I have shust de dings.

Blim: (*Springing up and hopping about.*) Good gracious! Oh, Lord! me leg is broken.

Peter: (*Laughing.*) Vot you leg vos proken?

Blim: Oh-h-h!

Peter: (*Laughing loudly.*) Vell, let me dell you von dings, Mister, uf your leg vos break so easy, get rid of it und buy a bair of crutches. How you vos feel now?

Blim: (*Groaning.*) A trifle better. Oh-h-h!

Peter: (*Imitating.*) Dot vos goot. So de room suit you?

Blim: I'll try it for a couple of weeks; here, I'll pay you in advance.

Peter: (*Rubbing his hands.*) Py shiminy! Dot vos de first sensible dings he say since he come in.

Blim: (*Drawing out a roll of bills.*) Here, I've nothing less than this hundred dollar bill; you'll have to change it for me.

Peter: Cerdainly, sir. Oxcuse me, for von second, dill I go up stairs und get de change oud of my drunk.

(*Exit Peter door S.E.L., Mr. Blimber makes a tour of inspection around the room.*)

Blim: There! I've got rid of one of them, anyway. Good gracious! If that Duchman only knew the note was counterfeit Whe-e-w! It's a fortunate thing he has the change in the house. I'll get it, go to the room for a little while to allay suspicion and then see if I can't pick up a few unconsidered trifles about the house. Ah! there he comes.

Peter: (*Aside, entering.*) I dond vos have enough change, so I garry dot hundred thaler bill to Krauz; he change it for me. (*Aloud to Mr. Blimber.*) Here vos your change, sir.

Blim: (*Counting money.*) It is quite right, sir. Now if you will show me to my room, I will rest awhile.

Peter: Cerdainly, sir; dis way, sir, cerdainly. (*Exit Peter, door S.E.R., Blimber following; as they go off, Murty pokes his head in at door R.F., seeing no one he enters, and comes down, cautiously.*)

Murty: I suppose, now, the ould Dutchman's gone out to get a drink av lager beer. (*Contemptuously.*) Lager beer! Divil burn me av I can understand people drinkin' lager beer whin they can git drunk so much quicker an' better on whiskey. I wonder av he heard me knock; begorra, I thought sure I'd batther the door in; av he didn't hear me he must be dafe as a post. This is a tidy sort av room, now; av the rest are anyways loike it, I'll not grumble, that's certain. Faith! I'll be like Paddy Burn's pig—laid up in lavender.

(*Re-enter Peter, S.E.R.*)

Peter: So; dot funny chap vos fixed. (*Noticing Murty.*) Halloo? vos you vant?

Murty: (*Scraping.*) I'm luckin' for a lodgings, sor.

Peter: Vell, ve vos keep dem sort of dings here.

Murty: A room for meself, Biddy, an' the childer.

Peter: Oh; ve vos have no rooms for children, here.

Murty: (*Scratching his head, aside.*) That's yer lay, is it ould cock? (*Aloud.*) Sure, the childer are very small, sor.

Peter: (*Shaking his head.*) No, no, nichts kinder.

Murty: An' there's only a couple, sor.

Peter: (*Slowly.*) Vell, only a couple, you say?

Murty: Yis.

Peter: Dot vos not so pad.

Murty: (*Slapping him on back.*) Av coorse not; an' I pay a month down.

Peter: (*Quickly.*) I dake it; den dollars.

Murty: (*Counting money.*) Here you are, thin. (*Aside.*) Faith! I knew that wud catch him.

Peter: (*Taking money.*) Beim Himmel! to-day I make gute geschaffen.

Murty: Well, I'll go now an bring the wife an' childer.

Peter: Ya-a-h; all right. (*Exit Murty, D.F.*) Und I go und dake ein glass beer. Ha, ha, ha! Peter Schlaginhauffen, you vos always a lucky feller; ha, ha, ha, ha! (*Exit Peter, D.F. Re-enter Mr. Blimber, S.E.R., cautiously.*)

Blim: So he's gone at last. Now, if I can only find his room and secure the contents of that trunk he spoke of a while ago, I shall have made a good haul to-day. Let me see. (*Crosses to L.*) I think he went in here before. Ha! the door's locked. Well, if he will persist in keeping his doors locked, I'm sure he cannot blame me for spoiling the mechanism. (*Picks the lock with wire which he takes from his pocket.*) It's open, and now we'll see what's to be found.

(*Exit Mr. Blimber, S.E.L., cautiously; a noise heard, as of voices outside, gradually increasing. The door R.F. is opened and a troop of eleven children stream in; Murty and Mrs. Rourke follow them; the children scatter about the room, quarrelling among themselves, and destroying and upsetting everything.*)

Murty: (*Charging among them.*) Will ye lave off, now?

Mrs. R.: Mary Ann, take yer paws off the furniture.

Murty: Av I lay hands on ye, Jerry, ye brimstone baste, I'll skin ye. Do ye moind that, now? I'm tellin' ye.

Jerry: I'd like to see you skin me.

Murty: (*Chasing him.*) Ye would, would ye? Well, me son, ye shall have that pleasure; skin ye, is it, ye vagabone? By me sowkers, I'll make mince meat av ye!

(*Murty chases Jerry, upsetting the children, falling over furniture, and stumbling everywhere. At last he runs against Mrs. Rourke, D.F., and she throws him into corner, where he falls. Enter Peter D.F. He stands aghast.*)

Murty: (*Sitting up.*) Tear an' ages! ye've disrupted me spinal chord. (*Seeing Peter.*) Oh, murder! There's the ould Dutchman.

Peter: (*Coming down violently.*) Donner und Blitz! vot vos all dem kinder make here?

Murty: (*Aside.*) Begorra, they're doin' their best to make a wrack av the place. (*Aloud.*) Sure, what should they be doin', sor, but be where their father is.

Peter: Vas? Dem vos all yours?

Murty: Av coorse.

Peter: Donner und Doria! dot vos too much.

Murty: Begorra, av ye had to kape them ye'd say so.

Peter: (*Violently.*) Vell, von dings vos certain, you shust get oud.

Murty: Fwhat?

Mrs. R.: Fwhat?

Peter: Get'oud!

Murty: Av I do, may I be—Luck here, now; didn't I pay ye a month's rint, down?

Peter: Oh, Moses! I vos forget dot.

Murty: Well, don't ye be forgettin' it any more; here I am, an' here I stay till me month's up.

Peter: But—

Murty: (*Boxing at him.*) Go 'long out o' that!

Peter: Wass? You do me dot in mine own house?

Murty: Yer lucky, av I don't do worse.

Peter: Vot? dot vos too much!

(*Makes a rush for Murty, who evades him. The children set up a howl and Mrs. Rourke*) *begins keening. Enter Policeman, D.F. He advances to Peter and taps him on shoulder with his club.*)

Police: Here, you're wanted.

Peter: Me? Vot for?

Police: Passing counterfeit money.

Peter: Va-a-s?

Police: Passing a counterfeit hundred dollar bill. Come along, now. (*Seizes Peter.*)

Peter: But—

Police: (*Forcing him towards door F.*) Come on, I say, or I'll club ye. (*A crash is heard, outside.*)

Peter: What's that?

Police: What's that?

Murty: Fwhat's that?

Mrs. R.: Fwhat's that? All together.

Peter: Donnerwetter! who vos dot in my room? (*Rushes off S.E.L. Noise of struggle heard; Policeman follows him and soon returns dragging in Mr. Blimber.*)

Blim: Let me go! what do you mean by this outrage!

Police: Come along; don't be uneasy in your mind.

Blim: (*To Peter.*) Is this the sort of a quiet lodging house I've got into?

Police: Don't worry about your lodging house; you'll find a fine stone building for your reception. (*To Peter.*) It's all right, my fine feller; you got the bill you changed at the grocery from this man, didn't you?

Peter: Ya-a-h.

Police: Well, it was counterfeit.

Peter: Vas gounterfeit?

Police: Yes.

Peter: Donnerwetter!

Police: You'd better come to the station house and try to get your money back.

Peter: Yes, I dinks so, doo; put pefore I go I have von dings to say mit dem folks dere.

Murty: Fwhat's that?

Mrs. R.: Fwhat's that? Together.

Peter: You dond vos clear oud?

Murty: Not a bit av it.

Peter: Oh, very well; den to-morrow I obens a Limburger cheese store here.

Murty: Hould on; for the love of St. Patrick give me me money back.

Peter: (*Giving him money.*) Dere! I thought dot vos settle it. Und now, mind vot I says, all of yous. I sthop renting out rooms—dot—is—(*coming down*) unless I can get dem nice ladies und shentlemans dot I see pefore me to gif a leetle encouragement to a boor Dutchman who has done his pest to make a success of DOT QUIED LOTGINGS.

A BURLESQUE ON
"UNCLE TOM'S CABIN"
by
HARRY L. NEWTON

CHARACTERS:

Uncle Tom, the original hard-luck story.

Little Eva, who finds it wearing on the constitution to die so often.

Topsy, our own idea of this famous character.

Simon Degree, who commits murder in the third degree and acts in any degree.

SCENE: Exterior setting, kitchen table and chair L., opposite second entrance.

COSTUMES AND MAKE-UPS:

Uncle Tom—Black-face, aged 45, gray-hair wool wig; flannel shirt, open at breast, showing red undershirt; no coat or vest; large red tie; white pants; patent-leather shoes and "loud" socks.

Little Eva—Character to be played by a large man. Blonde wig; very red cheeks; waist with low neck and short sleeves; ballet-dancer's skirt and tights; large bunches or knobs to be placed in tights to give limbs a grotesque appearance.

Topsy—Black-face; red-hair wig; dress with long train; large picture-hat; fan on chain and tied about waist; green stockings; sloppy shoes. General appearance on the SHE-may-have-seen-better-days order.

Simon Degree—Long black-hair wig; red chin-whiskers; slouch hat; linen duster; slap-stick instead of blacksnake whip. Speaks with strong Irish dialect.

SYNOPSIS: We are not responsible for what happens.

DIALOGUE: Curtain rises to music of "Bowery Buck."

(*Enter Simon Degree.*)

Degree: (*Advancing down stage, slap-stick in hand.*) B'gorry! 'tis a foine job I do be havin'. I have nothin' to do at all but lick the stuffin' out of Uncle Tom. (*Calls.*) Uncle Tom! Come out here; I want to beat ye up a bit. (*Strikes floor with stick. Enter Uncle Tom.*)

Tom: (*Walks slowly.*) Yes, mas'r, Ise comin, sah; Ise comin'.

Degree: Say, what's the matter wid ye this mornin'? Ye don't look happy.

Tom: Mas'r Degree, Ise done cast down dis mornin'. Ise afraid, mas'r, Ise afraid. Things ain't lookin' bright dis mornin', sah.

Degree: O, they ain't, eh? What things ain't lookin' bright?

Tom: Well, mas'r, dere ain't no use to try and keep it back. Ise only got eighty-four dollars dis mornin' and I wants to get a shave. (*Pulls out money.*)

Degree: Eighty-four dollars! Holy Nellie! How much does it cost to shave you?

Tom: Fifteen cents, mas'r.

Degree: Fifteen cents! Fifteen cents—and ye have eighty-four dollars?

Tom: Yes, mas'r; I ain't got enough for a shave and a tip, too. I needs fifteen cents for a shave. The tip I have. (*Shows money.*)

Degree: Poor old Uncle Tom! Here's twenty-five cents, and if ye have any change left bring me back a shampoo. (*Gives him coin.*)

Tom: (*Taking it.*) Thank you, mas'r. De good book says it am better to give than receive.

Degree: O, that's all right in some cases. For instance (*hits him in seat of trousers with slap-stick*)—now, I'd rather *give* that than receive it.

Tom: Yes, mas'r, you may be right; but I don't *see* the connection.

Degree: No, b'gorry! but you felt it. Now, see here, Uncle Tom, there's somethin' comin' off this mornin'. I'm goin' to hold an auction. I hate to do it, but you've got to be sold. Let's see yer teeth.

Tom: (*Opens mouth very wide.*)

Degree: (*Starting back.*) No, no! not yer breakfast—just yer teeth. (*Tom shuts mouth.*) Strip up those sleeves and show yer muscle. (*Tom rolls up sleeves, showing his white arms.*) Bad cess to ye! that's what comes from goin' in bathin' at South Haven. Come over to the block, ye blockhead! (*Grabs Tom and pulls him over to table.*) Where was ye raised?

Tom: Mas'r Degree, I don't want to be sold, Ise been sold long enough.

Degree: I ask ye again—where was ye raised?

Tom: On de South Side, mas'r.

Degree: Poor Uncle Tom! And did ye ride on the Illinois Central Railroad?

Tom: Yes, mas'r.

Degree: Then get up on the table. Ye've been *sold* so many times it won't hurt ye to get it again. (*Tom gets on table and Degree pulls off his red necktie and sticks it on wing. Tom's tie should be large and resemble an auction-flag when hung on wing. Calls to an imaginary crowd.*) Come on, boys! Come on, boys! Two can play as well one. Don't crowd too close. Stand back and ye can all see. Now, me good friends, I wants ye all to cast yer optics on this magnificent specimen of black humanity which stands forninst ye, and which I'm goin' to auction off this mornin'—

Tom: (*Interrupting.*) And don't forget to mention my patent-leather shoes, mas'r. (*Displays them.*)

Degree: Yes, that's right; he has patents on his feet, and it will take a long time for them to perspire—expire, I mean. Now, how much am I offered for this that stands forninst ye? Speak up, men, or forever hold yer peace. How much? (*Hand to ear.*) Dirty? Dirty it is—

Tom: (*Interrupts.*) No, mas'r, not dirty; I had a bath this mornin', sah.

Degree: (*Not heeding.*) Dirty dollars! Dirty dollars! Do I hear forty? Dirty forty-three? What's that? Dirty forty-three? Say, what do you think this is—a Siegel-Cooper bargain-sale? Do I hear forty? Forty I have! Forty! I'm bid forty! I bid forty-five! Forty-five! Forty-five—

Tom: Mas'r Degree, make it sixty-six; I can't play forty-five.

Degree: Shut up! Forty-five—and sold to Simon Degree. Come on, ye stick of licorice! Ye belong to me now—body and soul!

Tom: (*Getting down from table and kneeling on floor.*) Yes, mas'r, my body belongs to you, but my soul belongs to de janitor of our flat.

(*Degree raises stick to strike him, when Little Eva, from back of the audience, cries: "Stop! Stop, I say. I want to get off at Madison Street!" Eva comes down center aisle and climbs on stage.*)

Degree: Say, who be ye, I dunno?

Eva: Is it possible you don't recognize me? I'm Little Eva. I've died twice a day in Uncle Tom's Cabin shows for the past fifty-one years, and all I get is ten per and cakes.

Tom: (*Arising to feet. To Eva.*) Lord bless you, child; don't talk about dyin'. You just makes my old heart beat to beat the band. (*Bends over and Degree hits him with slap-stick.*)

Eva: O, Mr. Degree, please, *please* don't soak poor old Uncle Tom with that!

Degree: Pooh, pooh for ye! He belongs to me, and I'll soak him all I wants to.

Eva: But not with that—not with that! Take an ax—he deserves it. (*Puts handkerchief to eyes.*)

Degree: Aw, go chase yerself! Yer pullin' the wrong door-bell. On yer way! It's near time ye was dyin' agin.

Eva: Yes, I feel the habit growing on me, and if I am not careful it soon will be impossible for me to resist it. (*Yawns.*) I guess I'll have to go in the house now and get ready to make the women and children cry. They always cry when I die; I reckon it's because they want their money back. (*Exit, first entrance.*)

Degree: (*Looking after her.*) Poor *little* girl! How delicate she's gettin;!

Tom: Yes, mas'r; it's jest no use tryin' to keep Miss Eva here; Ise allus said so. She's got de Lord's mark in her forehead. She wasn't never like a child that's to live. I reckon she'll up and die befo' de act is over. (*Pulls out handkerchief, wipes eyes and then wrings water out of it. Have sponge wet with water inside handkerchief.*

Degree: Don't cry, Tom. It ain't no use; ye'll have all the black off yer face. Come, I'll take ye home with me and ye can lie down in me cozy corner and rest awhile.

Tom: Thank you, mas'r; you was allus good to me.

(*Exeunt, arm in arm, singing "She Certainly Was Good to Me." Orchestra plays cakewalk. Enter Topsy, doing cake-walk to music.*)

Topsy: (*At center stage.*) Gee, I feel lonesome. I haven't stolen a thing in five minutes. I'm gettin' too good. I'll have to get elected alderman, so I can steal all I want to and not feel lonesome.

(*Enter Eva.*)

Eva: Hello, Topsy! how are you?

Topsy: O, just middlin'. How's yourself?

Eva: O, rotten! Say, on the dead, Topsy, I don't think I'll live until the curtain goes down.

(*Orchestra plays slow music.*)

Topsy: Don't talk that way, Eva. Be a sport! Cheer up and die game. (*Reaches over and takes Eva's handkerchief.*)

Eva: (*Grabs Topsy's hand, takes handkerchief from her and slaps her on the wrist.*) There! take that, you cheap grafter! When you steal, steal something worth stealing.

Topsy: O, Eva, don't scold me! I have only one father and one mother and seven big brothers to protect and provide for me.

Eva: (*Feelingly.*) Poor little Topsy! (*Then sarcastically.*) O, you make me sick! Go and steal a couple of railroads and a ship-yard. Organize a trust and be a *real* thief, and don't go around swiping handkerchiefs. On your way! (*Waves hand. Exit Topsy.*)

(*Enter Uncle Tom, book in hand, intently reading.*)

Eva: Hello, cull! what's the book—dope? Put me wise to the Derby entries for next year, will you? (*Crosses and sits on table.*) Come over here, beau. (*Tom sits on table. Eva pulls out cigarette, strikes match on seat of tights, lights cigarette, puffs and smokes.*) Have a cigarette, old Bruno? (*Offers him one.*)

Tom: No, Miss Eva, I can't smoke any more cigarettes. Mas'r Degree done took away mah red tie. (*Points to it on wing.*)

Eva: The brute! I think he's just horrid! But say, August, what's the book, eh?

Tom: That, Miss Eva, am a dream-book.

Eva: A dream-book?

Tom: Yes, missy. Any time you dream a dream all you got to do is look in dis book, and you *won't* find de meanin' of de dream in de book.

Eva: Wonderful! Last night I had such a strange dream!

(*Slow music. Tom puts arm around Eva's waist, and Eva takes a wreath made of lettuce, celery, carrots, etc., from the inside of his waist and places it on Tom's head.*)

Tom: Tell old Uncle Tom 'bout your dream, honey.

Eva: (*Raising his face toward ceiling.*) Look in those clouds; don't they look like South Chicago smoke? (*Speaking dreamily to slow, expressive music.*) Last night I dreamed I was riding in a street-car—but ah, such a beautiful one! The seats were covered with satin; rich Brussels carpet was on the floor; overhead were clusters of electric lights, all encased in beautiful cut-glass globes. A string band concealed in one corner of the car gave out glorious music; noiseless waiters passed to and fro, serving free refreshments to the jaded and weary passengers. The wheels of the car gave forth no sound, and I did not feel the slightest jar or shock. The conductor, cap in hand, came into the car and, speaking in soft, highly cultivated tones, said:"Transfers to any part of the city." And then—and then—

Tom: And then you woke up.

Eva: Why, how did you know?

Tom: Because, missy, nobody in Chicago can get a-hold of a transfer to any part of the city—even in a dream.

Eva: You're right, Uncle Tom. Well, I guess I'll have to go and get ready to die. (*Gets down from table.*) This is positively my last exit before I go to heaven. (*Exit.*)

Tom: Poor Little Eva! She gets weaker and more delicate all the time. She ain't like no child that's to live.

Degree: (*Off stage.*) Uncle Tom!

Tom: Yes, mas'r.

Degree: Come in here and take yer cow out of the bath-tub; I want to take me bath.

Tom: Yes, mas'r; Ise comin'. (*Starts to exit, then pauses and looks toward where Eva made his exit.*) Poor little gal! I can see her finish. (*Exit. Cake-walk music. Enter Topsy, doing cake-walk.*)

Topsy: I have just ordered the undertaker to come and see that Eva does her getaway in first-class shape. As he is not here I will do a cake-walk out and look for him. (*Exit, with cake-walk. Enter Eva: walks with firm, heavy tread, and with shoulders thrown back, to center stage; lies down full length on floor.*)

Eva: (*Calling.*) O, Mr. Degree, where are you?

(*Enter Degree, running.*)

Degree: Fer the love of heaven, are ye goin' to croak agin?

Eva: Sure, Mike! I'm just about to shuffle off this mortal coil. (*Goes quickly to wings, gets long rope, brings it back and lays it on the floor alongside Eva. One end of the rope should be run through a pulley in the flies.*) There's yer coil. Go ahead and do yer shuffle.

Eva: (*Raising head.*) And Uncle Tom! Where is Uncle Tom? Poor old Uncle Tom!

(*Enter Tom, quickly.*)

Tom: Here I is, missy. Ise allus on time when you die, Eva.

Eva: It's awfully good of you, Tom, old chap; but it's too bad to trouble you so.

Tom: O, that's all right, Miss Eva. It's a pleasure to see you die—no trouble at all.

Degree: Shut up, both of yez! Yer delayin' the game. (*Takes end of rope and snaps it on Eva's belt.*) Now, Tom, give us a lift, and we'll soon have Eva up where she belongs. (*Both pull until rope is tight.*)

Eva: Hold on, you lobsters! I'm not dead yet—and besides Topsy should be here when I die.

Degree: Sure, and yer always right, little one. (*Puts finger in mouth and blows a shrill whistle.*) That's Topsy's cue to come on.

Eva: (*Lying back on floor.*) All set, men?

Tom: Yes, little missy; de pins am waitin' fer you.

Eva: Then good-by, Uncle Tom; good-by, Simon.

Degree: Are you dead now?

Eva: Why, sure—you Turk! Pull the rope.

(*Quick action from now till curtain. Tom and Degree both pull Eva up until he is clear of the floor: the music strikes up cake-walk, and Topsy enters with pan of lighted red fire. Tom and Degree pull Eva a little higher, then Degree yells: "Help! help! She's getting too heavy for us. Pull! Tom, pull!" Tom says: "Mas'r Degree, dis ascension looks to me like a frost if we don't get help." Eva says: "O, you guys make me sick! Why don't you get a couple of men on that rope?" Degree says: "A couple of men? B'gorry, we need a derrick!" Tom lets go of rope and gets directly in under Eva; Degree struggles to retain his hold of rope, and finally lets go, and Eva falls on Tom; both sprawl on floor, Tom underneath. Topsy still holds pan of red fire, while Degree grabs slap-stick and lays about him vigorously. Quick music. Curtain.*)

NOTES ON SOURCES

JOKES AND OTHER COMIC MATERIAL

Most of the jokes in this section come from a gagbook in my collection called "Uncle Cal's Manuscript No. 7." The gagbook is a simple typed manuscript of the "newsletter" sort, and is not dated or paginated. Some material is taken from several James Madison publications, including his "Budget," "The Comedian," and his "Weekly Service," all in my possession. One or two items come from two pocket-size joke books in my collection, both from a series called "New Stage Jokes." The comic song introduction was used by Julian "Greasy" Medlin and the parody of "My Indiana Home" by Dale Madden. Both were recorded by me in July of 1981 at Washington, D.C.

THE MONOLOGUE, THE PITCH AND THE LECTURE

Oranges, Anon., *The Boys of New York End Men's Joke Book* (New York: Frank Tousey, 1902), pp. 60-61.

Burlesque Oration on Matrimony. Ibid., pp. 57-58.

How Adam and Eve Turned White. Frank Dumont (ed.) *The Whitmark Amateur Minstrel Guide and Burnt Cork Encyclopedia* (New York: M. Whitmark and Sons, 1899), p. 86.

Stump Speech. Fred Wilson. "Stump Speech." Circus Broadside in the possession of John Towsen, New York City.

Troubles. Jimmy Lyons (ed.), *The Mirth of a Nation* (New York: Vantage Press, 1953), pp. 52-55.

Francis Wilson's Thrilling Wrestling Act. De Wolf Hopper (ed.), with F.P. Pitzer, *Comical Confessions of Clever Comedians* (New York: Street and Smith, Publishers, 1904), pp. 37-45.

Only a Clown. Recited by Johnny Patterson. Will H. Stowe (ed.) *New Comic Songster* (New York: New York Popular Publishing Co., n.d.),n.p.

Hamlet. Manuscript in the possession of P.A. Distler, Blacksburg, Virginia.

An Old-Fashioned Girl. Monologue used in chautauqua by Anna Blair Miller. Recorded in July 1981. Washington, D.C.

A Deck of Cards. Monologue used in tent shows and other forms of entertainment by Lois Madden. Recorded in July 1981, Washington, D.C.

Medicine Pitch; Candy Pitch; Greek Pitch; Used by Fred Bloodgood. Recorded in July 1981, Washington, D.C.

Josh Billings Lecture. Melville D. Landon (ed.), *Kings of the Platform and Pulpit* (Chicago: J.S. Ziegler and Co., 1894), pp. 80-94.

THE DIALOGUE AND THE BIT

Sidewalk Conversations. "McNally's Bulletin" (New York: William McNally, n.d.), pp. 46-47.

Remarkable Bravery. Dumont (ed.) p. 58.

Stupidity and Soldiers. Ibid., p. 59.

Messrs. Grin and Barrett. Harry L. Newton, "Messrs. Grin and Barrett" (Will Rossiter, 1903), pp. 1-11.

Interruption Scene. Tent show routine used by Lois and Dale Madden. Recorded in July 1981, Washington, D.C.

A Pack of Cards and the Bible. Lyons (ed.), pp. 174-176.

Buzzin' the Bee; Niagara Falls; Three Times Three are Ten; Izzy-Wuzzy; Prickly Heat. Manuscripts in the Chuck Callahan Collection. Hampden-Booth Library and Theatre Collection, The Players, New York City.

The Photograph Gallery. Bob Noell's Version. Brooks McNamara, *Step Right Up* (Garden City, N.Y.: Doubleday and Company, Inc.,1976), pp. 177-181.

The Bull Fight. Manuscript in the Chuck Callahan Collection.

THE SKETCH

School Days. Manuscript in Chuck Callahan Collection.

The Black Breach of Promise Case. Anon., "The Black Breach of Promise Case" (Chicago: The Dramatic Publishing Co., 1898), pp. 1-13.

Three O'Clock Train; Pete in the Well; Over the River, Charlie. McNamara, pp. 182-194.

Cluck's Sanitarium Scene. Manuscript in the Chuck Callahan Collection.

Dot Quied Lotgings. McDermott and Trumble, "Dot Quied Lotgings" (New York: Happy Hours Company, n.d.), pp. 3-8.

Burlesque of *Uncle Tom's Cabin*. Harry L. Newton, "A Burlesque on 'Uncle Tom's Cabin' " (Will Rossiter, 1903), pp. 1-12.